PRAISE FOR *F*

"Matt Lozano shows that the path to holiness is the furthest thing from dreary drudgery—in reality, it is a glorious adventure of living from what Jesus has already done for us on the cross. Rich in insights, personal examples, and practical suggestions, *Free to Be Holy* is a powerfully encouraging guide to spiritual growth."
—Dr. Mary Healy, Professor of Sacred Scripture, Sacred Heart Major Seminary

"Holiness and freedom: a match made in heaven. It has been my experience that most people don't really know or believe that they are or can be holy. 'Holiness is for other people, not someone like me' is a common sentiment. It's also true that many people believe that they are free but are in bondage. They have grown accustomed to it and don't realize there is another way to live. There are also some who for numerous reasons do not believe they can be free. In this book, Matt Lozano offers the reader a beautiful invitation to be both *holy* and *free*. Matt presents the call to holiness in a manner that is inspiring, convincing, attainable, and transformative. By sharing many personal stories, Matt makes it easy for readers to see in the path of holiness a road on which they will gladly walk. When we do begin this journey, we discover that it leads to a freedom that can only be found in God. I highly recommend Matt's book for all who wonder if perhaps God has more for them. He indeed does, and Matt makes this perfectly clear."
—Fr. Dave Pivonka, TOR, President of Franciscan University

"Readers will find this wonderful book to be both informative and uplifting. It provides important practical wisdom on how to identify and overcome the inevitable obstacles we all face on the road to holiness. But above all, this book communicates a deep conviction that the call to holiness is a joyful adventure, one filled with hope, because it is from beginning to end, the outworking of the fact of God's having set us apart for this purpose in and through his beloved Son, Jesus, our Lord."
—**Peter Herbeck, Executive Vice President and Director of Missions, Renewal Ministries**

"This book presents the most 'renewal of the mind' you can receive on this topic of holiness. I highly recommend the investment of your time in this book as it is sure to yield fresh revelation from God and an upgraded kingdom mindset in your identity in Christ."
—**Patrick Reis, Co-founder and Executive Director, Encounter Ministries**

"In his new book, *Free to Be Holy*, Matt Lozano offers the reader clear and practical steps for living a life of increasing holiness. Drawing from Scripture, the wisdom of the saints, and hard-won personal experiences, Matt gently casts a vision for growing in Christlikeness. *Free to Be Holy* invites all readers—whether new to the Christian faith or exhausted from trying to live a holy life—to let go of past failure and shame and embrace the hope of an identity rooted in Jesus."
—**Bonnie O'Neil, Executive Director of Alpha Mid Atlantic and author of *Chronic Hope* and *My Identity Is in Christ: Discovering the Freedom God Always Intended***

MATT LOZANO

Preface by Christopher West
Epilogue by Neal Lozano

FREE TO BE HOLY

Discovering Who You Are in Christ

Published by The Word Among Us Press
7115 Guilford Drive, Suite 100
Frederick, Maryland 21704
wau.org

27 26 25 24 23   1 2 3 4 5

ISBN: 978-1-59325-710-1
eISBN: 978-1-59325- 711-8

Imprimatur: +Most Reverend William E. Lori
Archbishop of Baltimore
March 9, 2023

Design by Suzanne Earl

Made and printed in the United States of America

Library of Congress Control Number: 9781593257101

For my wife, Jennifer, and our children Stephen, Anna, Micah, Jane, and Liberty. You fill my heart with delight.

Contents

Preface

Christopher West

As a Catholic author, I'm often invited to write forewords or endorsements for other Catholic books. I wish I could accept all the invitations I receive, but my own personal and professional responsibilities prevent that. Every so often, however, a book comes along that tugs at my spirit because of its importance for God's people. What could possibly be more important than growing in the freedom to be holy?

But what *is* holiness? Matt Lozano helps us discover that holiness is not first something we *do*. Rather, as we learn from Mary, it is first and foremost something we allow to be *done unto us*. It's first an opening to the utterly gratuitous gift of divine love, allowing its transforming power to enter the innermost recesses of our being. Only inasmuch as we have first been touched by so great a love are we then even capable of responding with love to the love we have received. *That* is holiness—love first given by God, received by the human person, and returned to God while being shared with others.

"

As Pope St. John Paul II

insists, the *I must*

"comes at the very end."

At the start is "the

great love of God."

When we forget that holiness is a gift, the call to holiness becomes an impossibly heavy burden—an intolerable list of *I musts*: *I must* believe this; *I must* fulfill this religious obligation; *I must* be faithful to this moral law. Authentic holiness is something infinitely *other* than a self-reliant "dutiful" life. It's not that we don't have responsibilities to fulfill. But to put them first is to put the cart before the horse. As Pope St. John Paul II insists, the *I must* "comes at the very end."[1] At the start is "the great love of God, who engaged himself in relationship to me. He came in my direction."[2] The beloved disciple understood this well: "In this is love: not that we loved God, but that he loved us" (1 John 4:10).

Here's a good way to understand this crucial point: we can never properly initiate the words "I love you" in relation to God. We can only say, "I love you, too." For "God's initiative of love always comes first; our own first step is always a response."[3] This is why, in the biblical analogy of spousal love, God is always the Bridegroom and humanity is always the Bride. It can't be the other way around. It's the Bridegroom who lovingly pours out his life-giving seed and the Bride who opens to receive that seed with her particular loving response.

The life-giving complementarity of the sexes is not merely a biological phenomenon; it's also a theological phenomenon that signifies the "great mystery" of Christ's love for the Church (Ephesians 5:32). In the truly loving union of husband and wife, we see a sacred icon of holiness itself. The *Catechism of the Catholic Church* observes that "holiness is measured according to the 'great mystery' in which the Bride responds with the gift of the love to the gift of the Bridegroom."[4] And here

"Mary goes before us all in the holiness that is the Church's mystery as 'the bride without spot or wrinkle.'"[5]

Scripture testifies that human holiness can only exist in the context of the most *intimate relationship* between God and each human heart. The Bible uses many images, of course, to describe this intimacy, but none is more prominent (and none more evocative!) than the spousal image. The second Person of the Trinity took flesh to espouse himself to us. He's inviting us to an eternal Wedding Feast in which the food we'll forever rejoice in is the Bridegroom himself! But it is not going to be a shotgun wedding. Here's where our freedom comes into play. "The Almighty awaits the 'yes' of his creatures as a young bridegroom that of his bride," as Pope Benedict XVI put it.[6] To give our "yes" to heaven's marriage proposal is to exercise the supreme act of human freedom—the freedom to be holy.

Like me, Matt Lozano is a layman who's been called to preach the gospel—which is to say, he's been called to encourage people to use their freedom to give their "yes" to heaven's marriage proposal. Both in his personal life and through his work with Heart of the Father Ministries, I have known Matt to be a genuine disciple of Christ. The keen insights you'll find in this book flow from his willingness to continue giving his own "yes" to the Lord in the midst of life's joys and trials. Packed with the wisdom gained from having accompanied countless people on their journeys from deep spiritual bondage into the freedom for which Christ set us free, I am certain that Matt's book will help you to access and partake in the Wedding Feast that is the Catholic Tradition.

May you be richly blessed as you pray through this book. And may it help you in being free to be holy!

Dr. Christopher West serves as president of the Theology of the Body Institute near Philadelphia and as professor of theological anthropology in its jointly sponsored master's program with Pontifex University. His global lecturing, bestselling books, multiple audio and video programs, and popular podcast have made him one of the world's most recognized teachers of Pope St. John Paul II's Theology of the Body.

Introduction

Ever since I was young, the lives of the saints have fascinated me. Their heroism, selflessness, and courage in the face of danger—and even death—drew me to them. At my Confirmation, I chose St. Sebastian as my patron saint, for two reasons. First, he was the patron saint of athletes, and at the time, I wanted to be a professional baseball player. Second, he was martyred twice! After being shot with arrows by the Roman authorities for his faith, St. Sebastian made a miraculous recovery and returned to the emperor Diocletian as a witness to his faith in Christ. The emperor then ordered him to be beaten to death.

I saw in St. Sebastian's story the qualities that I longed to see in myself. I wanted to be someone unafraid to tell the truth. I wanted to be strong and courageous—even if that meant standing alone. I wanted to be resilient and overcome opposition.

As I follow Christ, I can see that some of these qualities have become my own. I can be bold in my faith. I have overcome many trials, learned how to love, and been willing to take a stand for the truth. It makes me happy to know that in some ways, like St. Sebastian, I have grown to be more like Jesus through the grace of God.

The journey, however, hasn't always followed a straight line. I have many weaknesses. I struggle with anxieties, and I easily get discouraged. I experience stress during conflicts with others. When I am uncomfortable, I get defensive. I can be morose and irritable over little offenses.

It saddens me to know that, in some ways, I don't reflect Christ's love to others. And yet the Lord, in his goodness, is not finished with me.

The truth that God completely loves me is deeper than my strengths and weaknesses, and his love for me has awakened a desire to offer my life back to him in love. That's truly why I wanted to be like St. Sebastian: the Father's love placed a longing deep within my heart for holiness, a life lived for God. This is true for every single human person. We are made for the Father's heart and will only find our deepest fulfillment when we live out of the depths of God's love for us.

For some people, however, even the word "holy" triggers apprehension. They don't feel worthy, or they can't imagine that God would even be that interested in them to extend such an invitation to holiness. The expression "holier than thou" makes them think of holiness as a way for people to look down on others who seem less advanced in the spiritual life.

Worry about holiness can also lead people to live in constant fear of making mistakes or to operate under the notion that we must avoid every kind of desire. It can feel like a heavy burden or an unrealized expectation. You might feel that God is forever disappointed in you, and nothing you do will ever be good enough. Maybe you were given the impression that

God is holy, and therefore you better get your act together or face his wrath! Or you might think that holiness is the "no fun club," completely devoid of joy or laughter.

I don't know where you fall on that spectrum. Perhaps you've discovered the riches of God's mercy and grace, but you still don't want to approach the subject of holiness. Maybe you don't want to be stuck in a spirituality that emphasizes what we *do* over who we *are*. If that is your experience, then this book is for you!

Some of you might be attracted to the idea of holiness but don't know where to begin. You are inspired by the lives of holy men and women, but their experiences seem so different from yours. You think, "How could I, in my circumstances, possibly live a holy life?" Holiness seems like a distant goal: a finish line ever receding beyond the here and now. If that is your experience, then this book is for you, too!

Some of you have given up on holiness altogether. The habits you haven't overcome, the shame you feel over your failures, and the regrets you carry cause you to believe that you will never be holy. You see yourself as a sinner who is forgiven but definitely not a saint. If that sounds like you, then this book is *especially* for you!

Whatever perspective you hold, I have something to share with you that just might blow your mind! What if I told you that holiness is actually an *adventure*? That the pursuit of holiness is really the pursuit of joy? That holiness is about choosing the best, again and again, so that in living for God, we fulfill our deepest desires? Would you be interested in *this* kind of journey?

"

What if I told you that

holiness is actually an

adventure? Would you be

interested in *this* kind

of journey?

In this book, I hope to give you an understanding of what it means to be holy and of how to grow in holiness. What I will share is grounded in the Scriptures, the teachings of the Catholic Church, and my own experiences. Together we will journey to dispel the myths and misconceptions that can so often short-circuit the pursuit of holiness. Then we will build a foundation for what it means to live a holy life—free from insecurity, shame, and despair.

I want to offer you a foundation for holiness that is simple. I don't want to burden you with a long list of rules and expectations. Just the basics.

I pray that as you read and talk to God about the topics in this book, you will discover the freedom and courage to pursue a lifestyle that is a total "yes" to God. Let's get started!

Therefore, since we are surrounded by so great cloud of witnesses, let us also lay aside every weight, and sin which clings so closely, and let us run with perseverance the race that is set before us, looking to Jesus the pioneer and perfecter of our faith. (Hebrews 12:1-2)

CHAPTER 1

What Does It Mean to Be Holy?

When my kids and I go camping, I remind them that any stick they put into the fire has to remain in the fire. If they pull the stick back out, it is no longer just a stick but rather a fire hazard! The stick, when touched by fire, becomes *set apart* for the fire alone.

Were you ever taught the "five-second rule"? After five seconds on the ground, food becomes garbage and is no longer fit for eating. The food is now *set apart* for the ground, not your mouth!

When I was growing up, my mom had dishes that were for everyday use and fine china that she used for special occasions. The fine china had the same function as the everyday dishes, but the china was *set apart* for special occasions, like Thanksgiving, Christmas, and Easter. The rest of the year, those dishes were off-limits.

The Hebrew word for "holy" is *kadosh*, which means "set apart." *Kadosh* also means "sacred," "consecrated," or "purified." When we read about the way the people of Israel worshipped God in the Old Testament, we see that everything in the tabernacle—the utensils, the altar, and the priests—were made *kadosh* by the anointing of oil and the blood sprinkled on them. This act removed the guilt of past sins (atonement) and also marked the items as set apart to the Lord (consecration).

No thing or person that was made holy could be returned to ordinary service. The priests who were consecrated with blood could never go back to being ordinary Israelites. The dishes and utensils could never again be used for an ordinary meal. This might seem strange to a modern person. Yet we can imagine how blood would leave a definite mark on the priest's clothes, and the oil, which was spiked with five different spices, would be distinguished from other kinds of oil by its fragrance.

Do you remember those label makers people used to mark their tools and other property? One time my dad asked me to label some of his tools in the shed. I got a little carried away, and soon everything had "RETURN TO NEAL" written on it! Now, imagine that everything in the tabernacle, the tent where Israel worshipped, was marked with blood and oil. Everything in the tent belonged to the Lord.

So we can see from the earliest use of the word *kadosh* that to become holy meant to be cleansed from sin, marked as belonging to God's house, and set apart for worship. This fundamentally Jewish understanding of holiness helps us understand the good news about what Jesus has done for us on the cross in the new and eternal covenant. In the Letter to the

Hebrews, we read that Jesus offered himself as "a single sacrifice for sins" (10:12). In doing so, he made us holy:

> [W]e have been sanctified through the offering of the body of Jesus Christ *once for all*. . . .
>
> For by a single offering he has perfected *for all time* those who are *sanctified*. (Hebrews 10:10, 14, emphasis mine)

Jesus made an offering of his body. This offering dealt with our sins and set us apart for God. More specifically, Jesus' blood cleansed us from sin: "[H]ow much more shall the blood of Christ . . . purify your conscience from dead works" (Hebrews 9:14). That same blood makes us holy: "Jesus also suffered outside the gate in order to sanctify the people through his own blood" (13:12).

The Way of Sacrifice

All this might seem strange to you or make you feel a bit squeamish. You might be imagining a bloodthirsty deity demanding the violent death of Jesus in order to satisfy his anger. That is not at all what is happening here. Let's talk about sacrifice and blood for a moment.

Modern people tend to associate blood with violence and death; but for ancient people, blood represented life. In the Book of Deuteronomy, the Israelites were commanded not to eat the blood of animals because "*the blood is the life*, and you shall not eat the life with the flesh" (12:23, emphasis mine). So it is important to know that when we talk about the blood of Jesus, we are talking about the offering of his life.

We often look at the cross and see only the suffering and death of Jesus; thus, we miss the value of the life that he offered to God. You could say that we were saved by the death of Jesus, but it is more accurate to say that we were saved by the obedience of Jesus *through* death. If the violence done to Jesus saved us, then Pontius Pilate and the Roman guards would be our saviors! Instead, it was the offering of Jesus' life unto death, in obedience and union with his Father's plan, that rescued us from sin.

But why did Jesus have to die in the first place? To understand this, we need to take a step back and see the bigger picture. When Adam and Eve refused to obey God, all humanity experienced a separation from God that we call sin. Sin is an abuse of human freedom, a rejection of God, and the refusal to justly give to God what he is due. The result was a tear in the fabric of reality, bringing division and tragedy to all of creation. Our human nature became enslaved to the power of sin, hindering our ability to know and love God and other people.

The sacrifices under the old covenant atoned for sins in a limited and exterior way, rendering the person ritually "clean" and restoring them to participation in community life. However, these sacrifices were unable to bring about interior transformation, to break the power sin had over our human nature. As a result, no one could offer God what he deserved: a pure, undivided human heart completely offered to him in love. Sin darkened our minds and poisoned our hearts, causing a kind of spiritual death. We needed to be saved and set free, and only God could do it.

Years ago, I saw the theatrical version of *The Lion King* with my family. I was amazed at the athletic abilities of the actors who acrobatically danced and flipped across the stage. At one point, the actor playing Simba did several somersaults and flew high into the air. The crowd gasped as he landed awkwardly and fell to the floor. Immediately, the curtain closed, and the music stopped. After a few minutes, a voice announced over the loudspeaker, "The role of Simba will now be played by _____ (the understudy)." When the curtain reopened, everything was the same except there was a new Simba! The show continued, but someone new took on the role.

This moment illustrated for me what Jesus has done to redeem us. When humanity had fallen and become wounded, God rescued us by sending his Son to do what we could not. Jesus stepped into the role of Adam when he became man. He did it on our behalf. Because Jesus was truly one of us—embracing our human nature, he could offer a perfect sacrifice on our behalf. The offering of his body and blood, the life of a man perfectly united with God, atoned for our sin, reconciled us to God, and healed our human nature. Jesus conquered sin and death for us by remaining obedient to God unto death, thereby defeating sin's power.

A New Creation

Yet Jesus didn't simply save us *from* something (separation from God); he also saved us *for* something (a new kind of relationship with God). This all hinges on the Incarnation. You could say that Jesus died *for us*; however, the Word of God became man, so it is more accurate to say that Jesus died *as us*. Because Jesus was truly one of us—embracing our human nature—his perfect obedience mended the breach caused by sin and redeemed our humanity. He restored us to God and reunited heaven and earth in his own body!

The body and blood of Jesus offer us therefore a new humanity: in him we are "a new creation" (2 Corinthians 5:17)! When you were baptized, you died with Jesus and rose with him. His divine life and his righteousness became yours. The *Catechism of the Catholic Church* states, "The baptized have 'put on Christ.' Through the Holy Spirit, Baptism is a bath that purifies, justifies, and sanctifies."[7]

In faith and Baptism, we receive the life (the blood) of Jesus, which purifies us from sin, gives us a righteous standing with God (justification), and sets us apart as belonging to him (sanctification). We are truly born into a new life, freed from the power of sin and established as children of God. The blood of Jesus is a transfusion of grace, which means a "share in the divine life."[8] In other words, grace is transformative divine power.

Science teaches us that in the human body, blood has three powers. First, blood has oxygen, which animates the body. Second, blood has leukocytes, which destroy diseases. Third, blood has DNA, which is the power to reproduce cells.

In the same way, Jesus' blood animates our souls by giving us new life, a "second birth." Jesus' blood also destroys the disease of sin and cleanses us from unrighteousness. Lastly, the blood of Jesus reproduces, for it enables us to take part in God's nature as his sons and daughters.

"

When you were baptized, you died with Jesus and rose with him. His divine life and his righteousness became yours.

The next time you receive the Eucharist, try to imagine it as receiving a blood transfusion from Jesus! In it you receive God's power to animate, heal, and reproduce the life of Jesus in your soul. St. Faustina wrote this about the water and blood that flowed from Jesus' side: "Water which makes souls righteous. . . . Blood which is the life of souls."[9]

Jesus, the Source of Holiness

It is very important that we understand that it is Jesus' sacrifice that makes us holy. He is the reason we are holy. We can't depend on ourselves or try to be holy apart from him. We can't add to his gift or save ourselves.

It is not easy to depend on someone else to make us holy, but the truth is that we can't be holy without Jesus. Many of the great saints understood that the secret to growing in holiness is to rest completely in what Jesus has done and will do. I think of St. Joan of Arc, for example.

When Joan was put on trial for heresy and witchcraft, her accusers asked her if she was in a state of grace. The question was a trap. If she answered yes, her accusers would say that she possessed secret knowledge, which she must have obtained through witchcraft. If she said no, then she was admitting guilt of mortal sin. Her response confounded the accusers: "If I be not in a state of Grace, I pray God place me in it; if I be in it, I pray God keep me so."[10]

In this beautiful expression of faith, Joan acknowledged that it is the grace of God that makes us holy and draws us into holiness. Further, God's grace can be trusted completely to restore us when we fall into sin.

St. Thérèse of Lisieux is another model of this trust. She understood her own weaknesses very well. And instead of placing her confidence in her ability to overcome those weaknesses, she chose to believe in the power of God's grace to lead her into holiness. She wrote: "Your arms, then, O Jesus, are the elevator which must raise me up even to Heaven. To get there I need not grow; on the contrary I must remain little, I must become still less."[11]

A hymn by Anthony Showalter teaches us a similar trust:

> What a fellowship, what a joy divine,
> Leaning on the everlasting arms;
> What a blessedness, what a peace is mine,
> Leaning on the everlasting arms.[12]

These words were sung at nightly meetings by the citizens of Montgomery, Alabama, who boycotted the city buses following the arrest of Rosa Parks. Even as they made great sacrifices to end bus segregation in their city, they put their trust in God's grace to sustain them. When God calls us to do great things and make sacrifices, we must rely on his grace to give us the ability and strength to do them. We should entrust our pursuit of holiness to God's grace, not our abilities or willpower.

Being Holy versus Living in Holiness

I want to make an important distinction. Up until now, I have been describing holiness as *a state of being*. It is what you are because of Christ in you. Our trust and confidence in God come from intimately knowing that the sacrifice of Jesus was perfect. There was nothing lacking in what he offered the Father on our behalf.

Many of us struggle with feelings of inadequacy and incompleteness. The blood of Jesus *perfects* us. You might be averaging your "grade" in Christ: Jesus is a 100 percent, you are a 70 percent, with the result that you are an 85 percent when you are in him. Not so! You + Jesus = perfect obedience. Jesus gives you his perfect righteousness.

When you are in Jesus, there is nothing lacking in you. Charles Spurgeon wrote, "God is so boundlessly pleased with Jesus that in him he is altogether pleased with us."[13] Jesus' life restores us to a loving relationship with God, so that we can draw near to worship him. In Christ we are made holy. We are consecrated, and we belong to God. Even though we are often weak and sometimes half-hearted, we can learn to rest in him. We can trust that Jesus is enough.

You are holy.

You did not have to perform to become holy. Nothing you do could add to or subtract from the perfect obedience of Jesus, which speaks on your behalf (see Hebrews 12:24). There is no sacrifice more precious than the blood of Jesus, which purifies our consciences in the sight of God (see 9:14). In Christ you are truly "a new creation" (2 Corinthians 5:17).

Living in holiness is something different yet related to *being* holy. In Christ we are holy, and holiness is the *lifestyle that is appropriate to those who are holy*. Even though Baptism sets us apart as holy sons and daughters of God, we must cooperate with the divine life we have received in order to live in this identity. Holiness, therefore, is marked by an increasing measure of freedom from sin and the practice of virtues. Growing in holiness means that our choices, habits, and dispositions increasingly reflect that we belong to God.

Another way of understanding the state of *being holy* versus *living in holiness* is this: if being holy means being marked and set apart *for* God, then living in holiness is availability *to* God. See the difference? For example, when my wife, Jenn, and I made our marriage vows, we were consecrated to one another and entered the state of marriage. From that point on, no one would question our status as married. However, our status implies a lifestyle.

Imagine if after our wedding, Jenn and I never spoke to each other or lived together. Our lifestyle would be completely incompatible with who we are—a married couple. But Jenn and I do share our lives with one another, love each other, and sacrifice for one another, and thus our relationship clearly reflects our marriage covenant. The more we live in this way, the more perfectly we live out our identity as a couple united in marriage.

It is the same with being holy. The sacrifice of Jesus makes us holy, a status we could never earn for ourselves. Yet even though we have been made holy, we do not automatically live a holy lifestyle. Over time the grace of God will teach us how to live as our holy status demands.

A Free Gift

Jesus' offering of his body and blood, which makes us holy at Baptism and gives us the possibility of growing in holiness throughout our lives, is the demonstration of God's love for us (see Romans 5:8). Jesus taught his disciples: "Greater love has no man than this, that a man lay down his life for his friends" (John 15:13). When Jesus laid down his life for us, he revealed to us the greatest love. "God so loved the world that he gave his only-begotten Son, that whoever believes in him should not perish but have eternal life" (3:16).

It is important that we understand and rely upon the sufficiency of Jesus' sacrifice as the reason why we are holy and the basis for a life of holiness. Otherwise we will depend upon ourselves instead of him. We might think we need to add something to his gift of righteousness or that we need to save ourselves. This is a big mistake and one that the apostle Paul needed to correct in the earliest days of the Church. I believe that it is still a strong temptation for us today, one that appeals to our pride and self-reliance.

My friend Jessica, whom I have known since college, had a powerful encounter with God's love one night on a retreat during her senior year. She recalls:

> I had a career at the ready and plans for life in full motion, and I had no intention of being upended by religion, let alone by a man named Jesus. My vocabulary didn't include words like sanctification, redemption, or the like. However, God moved in my heart in ways that were unexpected and beautiful. At

the retreat, I began to understand that Jesus had offered his life for mine and that his sacrifice made me right with God. My debt was paid, and I was fully forgiven.

I whispered a fumbling expression of faith and surrendered my life to him. In a tender moment that is still vivid to me over twenty years later, I saw a picture in my mind. I was hanging on the cross, bloody and dying. Then the scene completely changed, and I saw Jesus looking at me. Tears fell from his eyes as he looked at me, still holding on to that cross. As he looked into my eyes, I could feel his gentle smile and a nudge in my spirit that whispered, "You don't need to be there; climb down. I have taken your place, and through me you are free to let go. I have paid it for you; you are mine, and you are loved. Let go."

My friend encountered the love of God that night through the redeeming sacrifice of Jesus. At the time, she had very little understanding of holiness. What she did know was that Jesus paid the price for her sins, and she did not have to pay for them. In short, she fell in love with the One who made her holy.

As I write this, I wonder how many of you reading this are holding on to your sins. Are you trying to pay your debts and prove your worth? I invite you to surrender to the love of God that takes your place on the cross and asks you to let go.

Prayer

Jesus, please forgive me for trying to save myself. I'm tired of trying to do it on my own. Thank you for laying down your life for me. I surrender to you. Thank you for your precious blood, which makes me whole. Amen.

REFLECTION QUESTIONS
(For Individual Use or with a Small Group)

1. What thoughts, images, or memories come to mind when you think about the word "holy"? What has shaped your concept of holiness?

2. Describe your approach to growing in holiness. How is it working or not working for you?

3. What does it mean for you that Jesus shed his blood to save you?

4. Is it difficult for you to trust in what Jesus has done for you? Do you ever feel as if you need to accomplish good things in order to be holy?

5. Being holy and living in holiness are two different things. Why is it important to know the difference?

6. Have you surrendered to the love of God? Or are you trying to earn his love?

CHAPTER 2

What Holiness Is Not

As I mentioned, one of the first issues the early Church needed to clarify was that the blood of Jesus was enough to make us holy. In addition to Baptism, some Christians taught that Greek believers had to be circumcised in order to become righteous and holy members of God's people. St. Paul, in his letters, particularly in his Letter to the Romans, courageously battled this idea. He understood what was at stake: if people put their confidence in something other than the blood of Jesus, they would stray from the grace of the Holy Spirit that was given to them in Baptism.

While male adult circumcision is no longer a controversy for the Church (thank goodness), the struggle over where we put our trust is still a major obstacle for many believers. Any approach to holiness that does not rest on what Jesus has done to make us holy can lead to very unholy consequences. The stakes are high. I know many people who have left the Church because they were wounded by an approach to holiness based on self-reliance or shame.

I had a friend in college who joined a cult. It was a small group of men and women who lived in a house near campus. They wore homespun clothing, and the men grew beards. The women would not speak to men outside the group. The cult recruited college students to join them, claiming that their group comprised the true tribes of Israel.

My friend, a new Christian, desperately wanted to live with a pure heart but had tremendous difficulty leaving his old life behind. He would fast and pray for weeks, worship and share his faith with others, but then he would crash, falling headlong into a weekend of immorality. The leader of the cult made an enticing promise, one that spoke to my friend's deep desire for holiness: "If you join us, you can live a sinless life." My friend completely bought in, dropped out of school, and moved in with the group.

Heartbroken and alarmed, my friends and I earnestly prayed and fasted. We made plans to meet with our friend, to try to persuade him to leave the cult. He was not allowed to meet with us alone, so the cult's leader joined us.

I distracted the leader by engaging him in discussion, while another friend spoke to the young man alone. She asked him why he was taking such a drastic step. He told her that he was just exhausted trying to live as Christ commanded and always failing. Now, under the strict control of the people he lived with, he had not sinned in weeks. Within the cult, he felt that perfection was possible.

This young man was passionate for truth, and he really wanted to live without compromise. He had concluded that the only way to grow in holiness was to surrender to the direction

"

It is tempting to reach for

a shortcut that replaces

your need to daily depend

on God's grace.

of other people who would protect him from his sinful desires. Impatient for change and tormented by shame, he chose to be controlled by people rather than transformed by God's grace.

This is an extreme example, but you might feel a similar frustration with your lack of growth in holiness. It is tempting to reach for a shortcut that replaces your need to daily depend on God's grace.

St. Paul wrote to the Galatians, "You were running well; who hindered you from obeying the truth?" (5:7). Paul had taught the Galatians to trust in the righteousness of Jesus, but then others came to say that the Gentile believers needed to be circumcised to be part of God's new covenant family. Instead of trusting in Jesus for salvation, they were entrusting themselves to the Law and their ability to follow it. It was as if someone had stepped into their path and led them down a new one without their noticing.

One time I was driving the streets of Washington, DC, without a map, and I decided to follow the car directly in front of me. After we turned past some cones and a barricade, he immediately stopped his car, put on his flashers, and informed me that I had just followed him down a traffic route that was off-limits—reserved for members of the United Nations. He politely pointed out the Secret Service agents who were ready to pounce on me if I didn't back out of there immediately! By blindly following what was before me, I had gotten myself in trouble.

Everywhere you look, the world will offer you a different path from that of relying on God's grace. Our pride will demand that we do it ourselves, that we make ourselves into something we can be proud of. We can easily forget about the life of Jesus inside us and depend instead on our willpower, strengths, and gifts. However, the shortcut so often becomes a dead end. We find ourselves right back where we started, exhausted and disappointed with ourselves. We experience shame and self-accusation.

In this chapter, I will identify three false approaches to holiness. They might seem like shortcuts to holiness, but they are really dead ends.

Performance

The first faulty shortcut is the performance approach. The performance approach is based on the idea that **our holiness makes us holy**. We think that our identity and our status as holy come from what we do.

In the movie *Forrest Gump*, many people ask Forrest, a lovable simpleton, if he is "stupid or something." His go-to response is "Stupid is as stupid does." In other words, Forrest believes that stupidity is not a trait but a habit.

This idea is attractive in our modern culture. It teaches us to define our own identities and preaches the endless possibilities of self-actualization and self-improvement. The idea that we can become holy by following a program could be used to sell a lot of books today.

I am not saying that you cannot *grow in holiness* through discipline and practice. What I am saying is that you cannot *become holy* by any means other than the blood of Jesus. A "program" will ultimately disappoint us, as it places our willpower as the source for our becoming holy. Then, when our willpower fails, so, too, will our sense of identity. We end up on a seesaw: today we're holy; tomorrow we're not.

Many of us go through this on a smaller scale every New Year when we make a list of resolutions. We feel great any day we carry through with whatever resolution we put our mind and energy behind. But when we falter or drop the ball in any way, frustration and negativity set in. Our self-image comes to depend on our performance.

The consequences are amplified when we believe that our performance—our ability to follow the rules and live out the obligations of our faith—makes us holy. It is Jesus himself—by his sacrifice, his grace, and his merits—who makes us holy.

When we are trapped on the treadmill of performance, the enemy can come in with accusations and lies about who we are (see the second false approach). When this happens, we need to be freed from our enslavement to our own performance. If we understand on a deep level that our identity is not wrapped up in what we do but rather in the Father's love for us in Jesus, then we can remain joyful and secure in our identity, even as we acknowledge our faults, shortcomings, and sins.

We need to be free from enslavement to our own performance. It is a dead end because it is self-focused. Do you really want your identity to be determined by how you perceive your latest time "at bat"? What if you instead identified with the faithfulness of Jesus? As the hymn by Robert Critchley says,

My hope is built on nothing less
Than Jesus' blood and righteousness. . . .
I dare not trust the sweetest frame
But wholly lean on Jesus' name.

On Christ the solid rock I stand.
All other ground is sinking sand.[14]

Our attempts to justify ourselves by performing are unstable ground. Jesus is a firm foundation that never fails. We can remain joyful and secure in our identity in him, while being honest and objective about our lifestyle. We can be convicted about our sin without letting it destroy our confidence in God's love or in who we are.

The performance approach was mine for many years. I often measured myself by whatever I had done lately. When I didn't see certain sins in my life, I felt proud and could believe that I was holy. When I failed, I felt miserable and thought that I was far from holy. I would crash, beat myself up, and beg for God's forgiveness, thinking that he wanted nothing to do with me. Only when I performed well could I imagine that God wanted to be close to me and could work through me.

God began to wean me from this understanding through a tender mercy. When I sinned, often I would want to hide from him and from others, but he wouldn't let me. God would put people in my path who needed love or something that I knew I had to give them. By his grace, God would use me in the most powerful ways during the times when I felt most useless and weak. In fact, there seemed to be more grace flowing through my life during these times than when I was feeling great about myself.

What was happening? I believe that God was showing me two things. First, that my performance could never change the love that he has for me or his ability to work in my life. Second, when I was more aware of my sin, I was also more willing to depend on him. I wasn't looking for an answer in myself but in Christ, who lives in me. I understood what St. Paul meant when he wrote, "For when I am weak, then I am strong" (2 Corinthians 12:10).

The opposite of Forrest Gump's response is true about being holy. Instead of "Holy is as holy does," it is "Holy does what holy is." Instead of asking ourselves, "What would Jesus do?" we should ask ourselves, "What does Jesus *in me* enable me to do?" **Our actions should be guided not toward who we want to become but toward who we already are in Christ.**

Out-of-Reach Holiness

A second false approach to holiness is the belief that **"I am not holy, but maybe someday I will be."** It is easy to fall under the sway of this approach, especially if you are a new believer and you start comparing yourself to others. When we sin, there is always the temptation to despair, and the accusation comes: "You are not holy."

Often we pursue holiness in an effort to overcome or escape from our sense of "not enough-ness." Self-anger is a fuel that burns out quickly. Our easily discarded resolutions can attest to this. In our shame, we identify with our sins and consider them to be our true nature.

"

Surrendering to his abundant grace and his all-sufficient righteousness is an inexhaustible source of joy, even amid our deepest failures and disappointments.

While it is accurate to say that we are sinners (because we do sin), **sin is not our identity** or our new nature in Christ. When we say, "Pray for us sinners" in the Hail Mary, it is important to understand that "us sinners" means "we who commit sins" not "we who are slaves to sin." If we identify with sin instead of the righteousness of God in us, we accept the omnipotence of sin, not the omnipotence of the blood of Jesus.

We do have a tendency toward sin, a weakness called concupiscence. However, our weakness is not our identity. Our identity is "God's holy people." In Ephesians, St. Paul exhorts us to keep on praying "for all the *saints*,"—the holy ones (Ephesians 6:18, emphasis mine).

Looking to ourselves, we will always find some flaw or other. For many of us, persistent sins become reasons to shrink back from the pursuit of holiness. We think, "I'm not good enough for God. I will never succeed." We give up on holiness before we even begin the journey.

Furthermore, we can always find another person who excels where we are weak, confirming for us the worst assumptions we make about ourselves. We doubt our dignity and our worthiness to receive love.

The answer is not in what we do or how we stack up to others but in Jesus, who lives in us. Our behavior will follow our expectations. Trusting in the righteousness of Christ will empower us to say no to sin and pursue a life of holiness. Surrendering to his abundant grace and his all-sufficient righteousness is an inexhaustible source of joy, even amid our deepest failures and disappointments. There is the beginning of true holiness—where the fire burns brightest.

False Standards

The third false approach to holiness is **setting yourself over and apart from other people.** Jesus warned his disciples to beware of the "leaven of the Pharisees" (Matthew 16:6). The Pharisees developed a form of self-righteousness that measured their holiness by how much they avoided the surrounding Greek culture, which they viewed as the source of Israel's sin. They added to the Law of Moses countless purity laws, governing with whom they associated, how they dressed, what they ate, and how often (and when) they washed their hands. Many of these laws focused on a superficial performance that looked superior yet only covered up sins and encouraged hypocrisy.

The Pharisees prayed lengthy public prayers, made gifts for show, and dressed to impress others. They tolerated injustice toward the poor, the breaking of vows, and the neglect of family members. Jesus described people who practiced such superficiality as "whitewashed tombs" (Matthew 23:27)—looking pretty on the outside but corrupt and decaying on the inside, where it mattered most. Jesus and his disciples openly violated the Pharisees' rules (by healing on the Sabbath, for example) to demonstrate God's kingdom and restore focus on the heart of God's law: the love of God, justice, and mercy.

No one likes to think of themselves as a Pharisee. It is important to know how tempting it can be to embrace the mindset of the Pharisees and make superiority to others our standard for holiness. Jesus told the story of a Pharisee who prayed, "God, I thank you that I am not like other men, extortioners, unjust, adulterers, or even like this tax collector. I fast twice a week, I give tithes of all that I get" (Luke 18:11-12). How easy it is to highlight our strengths in comparison to others' while ignoring our weaknesses!

When you make avoiding the sins of others your standard for holiness, you invite moral blindness into your heart. The standard for a holy life is Jesus. We must look to him as "the pioneer and perfecter of our faith" (Hebrews 12:2), because he is the source of holiness.

Another important lesson to learn from the Pharisees is that growing in holiness is not just about what you avoid—it is also about what you embrace. Yes, holiness involves purity, devotion, self-mastery, sacrifice, and excellence. But it is also worship, intimacy, belonging, friendship, and joy.

Some believers reduce holiness to self-denial. My sister-in-law Rachel had a conversion in high school, without much experience in Church life before that. She later wrote,

> When I first became Christian, so much of what defined me in my secular high school and college was that I didn't drink or have sex, as did so many of my classmates. I bought into the idea that what made me holy was what I didn't do, not what God did for me.

Now, it was very good that Rachel practiced what the Church teaches about drunkenness and premarital sex. However, an identity based on what we don't do or on being superior to others can become a source of religious pride. This in turn prevents us from living out the full truth about chastity and self-mastery. True holiness means saying yes to things that will draw us close to God as well as no to things that will draw us away from him.

Holiness, at its heart, is about availability to God—his presence, his voice, and his will. It means being detached from everything that keeps us from God but also being attracted to everything that brings us closer to him. Jesus modeled this lifestyle for us. Further, he testified that "the Son can do nothing of his own accord, but only what he sees the Father doing; for whatever he does, that the Son does likewise" (John 5:19).

Holiness isn't about us or how we look. It's about beholding Jesus, being transformed into his likeness, and reflecting his glory (see 2 Corinthians 3:18).

A Word about Sanctification

There is a process that transforms us as we pursue holiness, helping us be who we already are. It's called sanctification, and it's the working of God's grace to conform us to the image of Christ. Now, sanctification does not make us new creations; Christ living in us does that. Instead, sanctification reveals and helps actualize the new creation.

Thomas Merton wrote, "For me to be a saint means to be myself. Therefore, the problem of sanctity and salvation is in fact the problem of finding out who I am and of discovering my true self."[15] In a similar way, St. Catherine of Siena wrote, "Be who God meant you to be, and you will set the whole world on fire."[16]

For Thomas Merton and St. Catherine, **holiness is all about discovering and living from who we truly are in Christ. The** good works we do reflect the fact that we are Christ's workmanship. Though we have work to do, our identity is not found in our work but in who we are.

The most important motivation to "be holy yourselves in all your conduct" (1 Peter 1:15) is in these two imperatives: be holy because God is holy, and be holy because you are holy in him. This is the foundation we will build on in the next two chapters.

Prayer

Jesus, I desire that you be my standard for holiness. Lead me away from pride and superficial comparisons. As I look to you, the author and perfecter of my faith, help me trust in your holiness and who I am in you. Amen.

REFLECTION QUESTIONS
(For Individual Use or with a Small Group)

1. Is there a "shortcut" in which you are tempted to trust instead of in God's grace? What is it?

2. How can we escape the trap of the "performance approach" to holiness?

3. What is the danger in comparing ourselves to others?

4. Holiness involves detachment from sin but also attraction to God. What are some ways by which you might draw near to God?

CHAPTER 3

Holy like God

Years ago some friends and I drove into the beautiful and wild mountains of West Virginia for a weekend of rock climbing and camping. By the time we set up camp, it was pitch dark—so dark that I couldn't see my hand in front of me. When I got into my sleeping bag and looked up at the sky, what I saw took my breath away: millions of lights—of varying depth, size, and color—stretching as far as I could see. The stars, planets, and meteors were so present that I felt as if I were floating in space.

It was the same night sky that I had looked toward so many times in my hometown near Philadelphia. However, the light that surrounded me at home obscured the light from the stars, and I could only see a fraction of them. In the darkness of the isolated hills of West Virginia, my eyes could clearly see everything that I had been missing.

There's Always More to See

St. Paul writes,

> I do not cease to give thanks for you, remembering you in my
> prayers, that the God of our Lord Jesus Christ, the Father of
> glory, may give you a spirit of wisdom and of revelation in
> the knowledge of him, having the eyes of your hearts enlight-
> ened, that you may know what is the hope to which he has
> called you, what are the riches of his glorious inheritance in
> the saints. (Ephesians 1:16-18)

Reading this passage, I think about that moment when I saw
the night sky clearly for the first time. When I turn my heart
to God, the Holy Spirit can help me see more of God's breath-
taking beauty and endless majesty. It's as if the Spirit focuses
my gaze, blocking out the "light pollution"—the distractions,
self-occupied thoughts, and worries that keep me from experiencing the mercy, love, and presence of God.

In God there is always more to see. When someone is so
delightful and enjoyable that we cannot help but find our heart
drawn to them, we might say, "To know him is to love him."
Getting to know a kind, warm person activates our love for
them. Our *knowing* them increases our *love* for them. The
same is true with God: knowing him enables us to love him,
and loving him enables us to know him more.

According to St. Paul, you can only know God, in the sense
of relationship, with "the eyes of your hearts" that are "enlight-
ened" by the Spirit (Ephesians 1:18). This is more than a poetic

turn of phrase. The heart, for St. Paul, was not just the emotional center of a person but the center of the soul—comprised of mind, will, and emotions. Therefore seeing with "the eyes of your heart" means encountering God at the core of our being.

Scripture is filled with such examples. Jacob wrestled with an angel on his way back to Canaan (see Genesis 32:22-32), and Peter was confronted by Jesus' invitation to follow him (see Luke 5:1-11). Such encounters change us. Paul writes about this specifically in his Second Letter to the Corinthians:

> And we all, with unveiled face, beholding the glory of the Lord, are being changed into his likeness from one degree of glory to another; for this comes from the Lord who is the Spirit. (3:18)

A loving gaze toward God, with the help of the Holy Spirit, leads to transformation. We become more like what we see.

So far we have defined being holy as being *cleansed, marked, and set apart for God*. We also defined holiness as *a lifestyle of availability to God*. In this chapter, we need to address the question "How is God holy?" The answers to this critical question will help us understand the Lord's instruction to us: "You shall be holy; for I the LORD your God am holy" (Leviticus 19:2).

How Is God Holy?

The word "holy," when applied to God, does not mean "set apart *for*." It means "set apart *as*." God is not set apart for himself; he is set apart as himself. Another way of expressing this is to say that God is totally other; he is completely unique in himself.

Neither is "holy" a way to describe only God's moral purity. Rather, it describes the excellence of his being in every way. It is not simply one of his many attributes, like his love or his wisdom, but rather a descriptor of all his attributes. God's love is holy, his wisdom is holy, and his beauty is holy. God is incomparable to everything else in all creation. He is *set apart*.

I named one of my sons Micah, which in Hebrew means "Who is like the Lord?" It is a question that invites wonder because at its heart, the answer is, quite simply, no one. No person and no thing is quite like God.

A term that helps us understand God's holiness is "*transcendent majesty*"—an otherness that has no measure. God is not just preeminent, meaning the greatest of all. He isn't simply the greatest being in all creation, for example. Being "transcendent" means that he is infinitely greater than all. God is infinitely beyond creation.

Meditating on God's transcendent majesty is like taking a dive into a bottomless sea or floating through space—: you can't fully grasp it, but you can experience its power when you immerse yourself in it. That is why St. Paul described his mission this way: "To me, though I am the very least of all the saints, this grace was given, to preach to the Gentiles the unsearchable riches of Christ" (Ephesians 3:8).

God's transcendent majesty does not imply that God is distant from us. In fact, his majesty means that his glory fills the whole earth, and his power holds everything, including us, together. Preaching the "unsearchable" (also translated as "*boundless*") riches of Christ did not cause St. Paul to despair. Rather, the revelation of Jesus proved to be a source of endless wonder, amazement, and joy.

When St. Paul encountered the resurrected Jesus, it completely blew the lid off his limited understanding of God's wisdom and plan for the world. His goal was no longer to contain or define the limits of God. Instead, his desire was that Christians would be "filled with all the fulness of God" (Ephesians 3:19).

Contemplating the Attributes of God

It can be helpful to read quality works of theology and Scripture so that you can meditate on the attributes of God. Taking time to meditate on his omniscience, omnipotence, existence, unity, glory, and benevolence can be a doorway to deep contemplation—another way of keeping a loving gaze upon God with the eyes of your heart. With the Holy Spirit's help, you will have power to comprehend more of him than your mind alone can behold.

St. Thomas Aquinas spent his life considering many challenging questions about God and writing thoughtful responses in his masterpiece, the *Summa Theologica*. However, after a powerful experience of God's presence at Mass, he stopped writing and said, "I can do no more. Such secrets have been revealed to me that all I have written now appears to be of little value."[17] St. Thomas's gaze enabled him to see more of God, and it brought enlightenment to his years of meditation.

A loving gaze upon God can happen in a variety of settings. I might be standing before the ocean or looking up at the night sky. Sometimes it is in adoring Jesus in the Blessed Sacrament. Sometimes I go for a run while listening to my favorite worship music, and I can't help but lift my voice in song and raise my hands to the sky. In these moments, I can feel the expansion of my heart as I perceive the majesty of God.

The truth is that God is everywhere, and there is no place or circumstance in which we cannot turn our hearts toward his presence. Even a moment of silence in the middle of a busy day can bring us to the throne of God.

Revelation 4 describes "four living creatures" (cherubim) who surround the throne of God (4:6). Isaiah 6 describes the "seraphim" (which means "burning ones"), who fly above the throne (6:2). These creatures have been specifically designed to exist in the presence of God and to take in his glory. The cherubim, for example, are covered with eyes. Yet the seraphim need to shield their eyes from the power and beauty that emanate from God; they use their wings to cover their faces and their feet (see Isaiah 6:2). In awe and wonder, they cry out ceaselessly:

Holy, holy, holy is the LORD of hosts;
the whole earth is full of his glory. (6:3)

At the sound of their voices, the doorways to God's Temple shake, and the Temple fills with smoke (see Isaiah 6:4).

The creatures' repetition of the word "holy" is known as an *emphatic triplet*. For the Hebrews, repeating a word placed emphasis on it. Jesus would often say, "Truly, truly, I say to you" to emphasize the importance of his teachings. So the emphatic triplet "holy, holy, holy" emphasizes the transcendent majesty of God. It's not that the creatures are declaring God's holiness by degrees—that is, "Holy, holier, holiest!" Instead, they exclaim their overwhelmed wonder.

And they do this ceaselessly, with no loss of intensity, no familiarity, no boredom. They exclaim a truth that words can only approach but never contain. The *Catechism of the Catholic Church* says, "Our human words always fall short of the mystery of God" (42).

The emphatic triplet is also a very human expression of awe. Years ago I was watching a football game between the Philadelphia Eagles and the New York Giants, a game now famously named "The Miracle at the Meadowlands II." My team, the Eagles, who were down by twenty-one points, made an unbelievable comeback, scoring four touchdowns in the last eight minutes of play. The last score was a punt return, and the Eagles won the game in the very last second. The television commentator, who typically has a lot to say, could only repeat, "Oh! Oh! Oh!" as the final touchdown was scored. His emphatic triplet was an expression of wonder.

It seems that when we see something incredible, we tend to repeat ourselves. I can find myself doing this when I'm speaking to someone important or someone I greatly admire. Now, imagine how starstruck you might be in the presence of the almighty King!

Steve Jobs, the founder of Apple, was renowned for his picky and critical gaze. His obsession was making technological goods that were seamless and beautiful. When his engineers showed him a prototype, no matter how impressive, his first response was always "It's terrible." (He actually used a less polite expression.) A billionaire, Jobs would live for months without a couch in his living room until he found one that met his specifications. He would not sacrifice his vision or expectations, no matter the cost. In adhering to such exactitude, he and his teams revolutionized several industries.

Jobs spent the final moments of his life staring into the eyes of his children. He looked at them for a long time, then at his wife. Finally he gazed past them, into the distance. "Oh, wow," he said. "Oh wow. Oh wow."[18]

What did Steve Jobs see in his final moment? An angel? The Lord? What met his gaze to fill him with such wonder that he could only repeat, in an emphatic triplet, the word "wow"? What captured his demanding heart, which had spent a lifetime searching for beauty?

We can only guess. But his words give us insight into the amazement expressed by the seraphim in the presence of God. Even the creatures with the highest capacity for experiencing God are overwhelmed by his holiness. They cry out, "Holy," declaring his praise.

Transformed by Encounter

When I was in high school, my friend Kevin contracted meningitis and fell into a coma. He spent weeks in the intensive care unit as my friends and I prayed for his healing. Kevin was a popular student who played goalie for the soccer team;

he was also the starting pitcher for the baseball team. He had recently attended a fall weekend retreat with me and other friends, where he had heard the gospel message. He wasn't ready at that time to become a follower of Jesus. In fact, our youth leader had to confiscate some beer from Kevin's bags!

Thus Kevin had been on our prayer list for many months before he fell ill. We had prayed that God would intervene in his life to bring about his conversion. God answered those prayers in a way that we never expected.

I'll never forget the moments I spent with Kevin after he came out of the coma. His eyes seemed bluer than before. His face seemed radiant—almost childlike. Every time he tried to speak about his experience, tears filled his eyes. He tried to describe an encounter he had with Jesus while his organs were shutting down and it wasn't clear that he would live. He tried to describe the beauty of Jesus and the brightness of the light that surrounded him. He tried to share about the quality of Jesus' voice and the gentle words Jesus spoke to him.

As Kevin shared, I could sense how intense his longing was to return to the presence of the Lord and how grateful he was to experience God's mercy. Kevin would never be the same.

Most of us have never had that kind of encounter, but we are capable of seeing the Lord in different ways. We mentioned earlier that St. Paul teaches that a loving gaze of the heart toward God leads to transformation. You cannot be in the presence of God and remain the same. Spend time in the thrice-holy God's presence, and you will become like him. When you encounter the greatness of the Lord, you bend toward him, as does a sunflower toward the sun.

"

When you encounter

the greatness of the Lord,

you bend toward him,

as does a sunflower

toward the sun.

This experience is what we call "the fear of the Lord." We respond to what we see with reverence and acknowledgment of God's greatness. It is not terror, which is a fear that causes us to flee. The fear of the Lord is a sense of *trembling wonder*.

The word for "worship" means "to bow." When we respond in the fear of the Lord, our hearts align with reality: we acknowledge God's greatness, beauty, and majesty, and we acknowledge our dependence on him for everything. Our relationship to the One who created us and our relation to all creation become clear in these moments.

A great example of this is the faith of the Roman centurion who asked Jesus to heal his servant. This centurion was a man intimately familiar with authority. He was under the authority of his superiors, and he had authority over a hundred men. When he gave an order, it was done immediately, for the authority he carried came from the emperor himself.

The centurion saw something in Jesus—something no one else had seen. He recognized that Jesus had authority over sickness, and therefore he knew that Jesus did not have to come to his house to heal his servant. If Jesus said the word, it would be done. So when Jesus offered to come to his house, the centurion replied, "Lord, I am not worthy to have you come under my roof; but only say the word, and my servant will be healed" (Matthew 8:8).

Jesus was astonished at the centurion's faith, for this man "saw" more in Jesus than anyone in Israel had seen. The centurion saw greatness in Jesus, and he bowed toward it. Jesus replied to the man, "Go; let it be done for you as you have believed" (Matthew 8:13). The centurion's servant was healed in that very moment, and Jesus' power to heal was displayed in a new and glorious way.

How would you like to astonish Jesus with your faith? Faith grows as we look upon the holiness of God. When we bend toward him, the problems we face don't seem so impossible. God becomes exalted in our thoughts as we seek him for solutions. We learn to trust him more deeply when we know how holy he is.

Transformation as Repentance and Surrender

As we gaze upon God and are transformed into his image, some things that are not holy in us will be exposed by his light. Many times when I am with God in prayer or at Mass, I become aware of a judgmental attitude or a resentment that I have toward a friend or relative. Sometimes I remember a harsh word that I spoke in anger or a lack of love and gratitude for the people in my life. As I draw near to God, he gives me the gift of repentance.

Repentance is a change of mind that leads to a change in action. I can take my sins to Confession and receive God's grace to set a different course. Jesus taught his disciples that when they brought their gifts to the Temple, if they remembered that they had sinned against someone, they should go and be reconciled first, then offer their gift (see Matthew 5:23-24). When we draw near to God, our sins can be exposed. Repentance enables us to "lay aside every weight, and sin which clings so closely" (Hebrews 12:1).

God's presence is a refining fire. He wants us to be free from everything that prevents us from seeing him. Seeking him can be very practical and specific, but sometimes it can be uncomfortable. Psalm 24 reads,

Who shall ascend the hill of the LORD?
And who shall stand in his holy place?
He who has clean hands and a pure heart,
who does not lift up his soul to what is false,
and does not swear deceitfully.
He will receive blessing from the LORD,
and vindication from the God of his salvation.
Such is the generation of those who seek him,
who seek the face of the God of Jacob. (24:3-6)

When we enter the presence of a holy God, the uncleanness of our hands or the impurity of our hearts may be exposed. However, God does not want us to draw back in shame or fear. Jesus has already provided the gift of righteousness so that we can stand in God's presence. He wants us to repent of our sins, forgive others, and renounce our idols so that we can see him more clearly.

Remember that it is with the eyes of the heart that we see God. Purity of heart, wholehearted devotion, and availability to God: these enable our sight. Without holiness we see God through a lens that is smudged, scratched, and misshapen.

For example, when I get angry, usually because of my circumstances, I am tempted to believe that God is distant, cold, or uncaring. I sometimes withdraw my heart from him as a result of my false images of him. I then try to fill my sadness with distractions, work, or pleasure. When I do this, I am creating a false image of God, lowering him to the level of my experiences.

When my "pity party" comes to an end, I repent, open my heart again to God, and surrender. I discover that God was always with me, drawing close to me in my pain. When I recommit myself to walking in holiness, my sight is restored so that I can worship him.

Jesus calls us to leave behind everything that hinders us from seeing and encountering his presence.

Three Ways to See God with the Eyes of Our Hearts

St. Paul makes it clear that we see God "dimly," as "in a mirror" (1 Corinthians 13:12). A mirror in Paul's time was a polished piece of glass that did not reflect a clear image. Yet even with an imperfect view, God's glory is reflected in us, and his image shines from our faces (see 2 Corinthians 3:18). If you want to receive more of the glory of God, I encourage you to seek three things that will help you.

First, become rooted and grounded in God's love. Meditate regularly on the truth that God has forgiven you and that nothing can separate you from his love. This is a foundational truth but one from which we can easily get distracted.

You can also meditate on the truth that in Jesus, God is pleased to dwell with us. He desires you to experience his presence! Jesus knows intimately what it means to be like us—to suffer and to weep. He humbled himself and became obedient to death on a cross for us. His transcendent majesty does not diminish his love or his desire for us.

Second, ask for the power of the Holy Spirit to take you more deeply into the mystery of God's love. Even our best thoughts and prayers fall short, and I know how difficult it can be to remain focused during times of prayer. I take comfort knowing that even St. Paul acknowledged that prayer is difficult. He wrote,

> Likewise the Spirit helps us in our weakness; for we do not know how to pray as we ought, but the Spirit himself intercedes for us with sighs too deep for words. And he who searches the hearts of men knows what is the mind of the Spirit, because the Spirit intercedes for the saints according to the will of God. (Romans 8:26-27)

Even though we are weak in understanding, ability, and strength, the Holy Spirit can help us. The Spirit knows the mind of God, so he can bring us revelation that we could never acquire on our own. In addition, the Spirit intercedes for us by joining with our prayers. He draws out sighs and longings from the depths of our souls, and he does so with God's perfect will in mind.

When we pray—even if we are restless, distracted, or clueless about what to pray for—we make ourselves available to the Spirit so he can spiritually "stretch" us. The groaning and longing we experience in prayer create in us a deeper well into which God will pour himself.

Third, spend time with other people who are seeking God. We need the whole Church, all the holy ones who share a vision of the holy God. Share with others what you are discovering, and listen to them as they share or pray. Other people will often see something in their vision of God that you do not.

One of my favorite things is getting together with friends or family members and reading a Scripture passage together, then taking time to make comments and share thoughts about its meaning. I am amazed at how many different thoughts and perspectives you can have about just a few lines of God's word.

The following prayer from Ephesians is a summary of these three practices. As you read the prayer, see how the three practices work together to help draw us into the presence of God:

> [I pray that you] may have power to comprehend with all the saints what is the breadth and length and height and depth, and to know the love of Christ which surpasses knowledge, that you may be filled with all the fulness of God. (3:18-19)

Seeing God for who he is fills us with his fullness. True holiness begins with such a vision of God, for it awakens our faith, inspires repentance, and gives us a sense of awe and reverence. It gives us a vision of who we are created to be, for we are made in God's image.

God's presence helps us understand who we are. In the next chapter, we will discover the power of our identity in Christ.

Prayer

Lord, open the eyes of my heart so that I might see more of you. I want to be transformed by your presence and your love. As I draw near, show me anything that clouds my sight, that I may turn from it. Give me the grace to seek your face.

REFLECTION QUESTIONS
(For Individual Use or with a Small Group)

1. When was the last time something left you speechless in awe and wonder?

2. Ask God to enlighten the eyes of your heart. As you spend time gazing, what do you see?

3. Do you need to repent of any false views of God that you have held?

4. Make a plan to devote some time each day meditating and adoring God. When and where are the best times and places for you to be with him?

CHAPTER 4

You Are Holy

Since Christians are reclothed in Christ Jesus and re-freshed by his Spirit, they are "holy." They therefore have the ability to manifest this holiness and the responsibility to bear witness to it in all that they do. The apostle Paul never tires of admonishing all Christians to live "as is fitting among saints" (Ephesians 5:3).

—Pope St. John Paul II, *Christifideles Laici*, December 30, 1988, 16.

"Honestly, I'm not sure I really know who you are these days." My father's words caused my heart to sink. I was in eighth grade, and he had just found out that I had been doing something that I was too ashamed to admit. As I tried to lie about it, he called me out, essentially asking the question, "Who are you?"

The truth was, it did seem as if there were two "Me's." There were parts of my life that were morally excellent but other parts that were contradictory.

As I sought to grow in holiness, one of the most painful and frustrating battles for me was with lust. When I was a teenager, I was awakened to lust as a means of escape and a false attempt to soothe the loneliness in my heart. At the same time, I was deeply ashamed of my sins. I hated them, but I also hated myself. I saw my desires and my heart as a burden to be managed. I was painfully aware of both the call to walk in holiness and my inability to walk away from sin.

In moments of guilt and shame, I experienced a crisis over my identity: "What am I? Am I a sinner or a saint?" Depending on what day you asked me, I might tell you that I was one, the other, or both. Which was the real me? The selfish, escape-seeking person I was on some days? Or the virtuous, prayerful, and generous person that I was on other days?

My heart longed for greater integrity, for some sense of wholeness in my character that I found elusive. I was, quite simply, stuck. My approach to holiness was rooted in my performance. My efforts to overcome sin and practice virtue were desperate attempts to prove my worth, demonstrate that I was good, and, at the same time, escape the relentless inner accusation that I was not. The pain of disappointment with myself and the roller coaster of emotions that followed whenever I failed exhausted me.

What I needed wasn't another programmatic approach to self-improvement; I had tried many. Rather, I needed a shift in the way I viewed myself.

What held me back most in my pursuit of holiness was a self-perception that reinforced my sins. I thought that when I sinned, it was an expression of my true self. I would berate myself: "I'm horrible. I'm not like Jesus." I was trapped in a cycle of shame and self-hatred, followed by a period of striving and performance that always ended in failure. I was trying to run from myself because I believed that, at my core, I was wicked.

I was identifying myself with what St. Paul called my "flesh," which is simply human nature under the power of sin. Trying to overcome your flesh (inclination to sin) with your flesh (the force of your will alone) is impossible.

I thought that my sin was evidence that I was not holy and that I needed God to change me into someone else before I could become holy. I would pray earnestly, "God, create in me a clean heart!" Then one day, to my surprise, God responded, *"I already did. Start living from it."*

Thus I realized this fundamental truth: *the clean heart I had been praying for was already present and available for me to live from.* When I came to this understanding, it completely changed the game for me. God was inviting me to live by the Spirit he had already given me and to identify with my new nature in Christ.

Guilt versus Shame

Guilt is a good thing. It is the awareness that we have done something wrong; it comes from a healthy conscience. However, when we identify with our flesh, it opens the door to an unholy and unhealthy sense of shame. This shame is a sense of worthlessness, self-criticism, and hopelessness, combined with embarrassment and the urge to hide ourselves.

The root of shame is a belief that something is deeply wrong, not just in what we have done but in *who we are*. Shame responds to sin by saying, "This is really who you are, an unlovable person." When we are trapped in shame, it gives the enemy of our souls an advantage over us. Unholy shame is really an agreement with the devil, whom heaven refers to as the "accuser of our brethren" (Revelation 12:10). Shame is often what keeps us from bringing our sins and ourselves to the Lord for mercy and healing. On another occasion, I prayed, "God, I am such a horrible sinner." He responded, "*Why are you identifying with what my Son died to separate you from?*" In that moment, I realized that I was listening to the voice of shame instead of the truth of the gospel.

When I stopped identifying with my flesh, it released me from the power of shame. Instead of wallowing in self-condemnation and despair, I could look objectively at my sin for what it was. When I could see my sin as an "it" instead of "me," I could freely enter repentance—the process of turning from sin and toward God. I could bring my sin to God in Confession, name it, and ask God for the grace to turn from it. In doing so, I invited the Holy Spirit to lead me and change the way I thought. I was taking up the identity given to me at Baptism, by which I was washed in the river of God's grace and born into new life.

Many believers think that they can shame themselves into holiness. They believe that they can use their feelings of disgust and self-hatred to motivate them to change their lives. The truth is that you can't. Self-hatred will only fuel you for a short time. The way to holiness is to be unconditionally loved by a holy God.

"

When I am aware

that God truly loves me

as I am—with all my

flaws and failures—I

begin to have hope.

God's love will transform your heart, your identity, and your perspective. The love of Christ will set you free from your self-focus and allow you to see others as the objects of his all-encompassing love (see 2 Corinthians 5:14). As St. John the apostle wrote, "We love, because he first loved us" (1 John 4:19).

When I am aware that God truly loves me as I am—with all my flaws and failures—I begin to have hope. I can see myself as a saint who wrestles with sin, not a sinner who is trying to make himself holy. As Pope St. John Paul II said at the 17th World Youth Day in Toronto, "*We are not the sum of our weaknesses and failures*; we are the sum of the Father's love for us and our real capacity to become the image of his Son."[19] Take those words into your heart, and speak them over yourself. They contain the truth about who you are.

I find this illustration helpful. Imagine you are walking on the beach, and you step on a nail, which gets stuck in your foot. If you saw someone and asked them for help, you wouldn't say, "Help me; I am such a nail!" Instead, you would say, "There is a nail in my foot. Please help me get it out!"

We don't identify ourselves with the cause of our pain and say, "I am such a worthless nail!" Why, then, do we so often relate to sin in this way? Identifying with our sin keeps us from seeking help. It drives us to make excuses or justify our behavior: "It's not that bad; it's more of a thumbtack than a nail."

Identifying with sin leads us to shame, which ultimately isolates us from God and others. We think, "No one can help me; it's hopeless."

Grace and the Flesh

While it is true that we have the capacity for sin, as well as a tendency toward it, **sin is not our identity**. God's grace is more powerful and abundant than sin. By God's grace the life of Jesus dwells in us. And "where sin increased, grace abounded all the more" (Romans 5:20). The life of Jesus *in us* makes us "a new creation" *in him*, and we are no longer slaves to sin (2 Corinthians 5:17; see Romans 6:6). Our flesh, though it remains with us, is dead. Our new life in the Spirit is alive. One is powerless; the other is powerful. One is what you thought of you; the other is you.

It is important to note here that the word "flesh" (*sarx*) in Scripture does not refer to your body. The Church has always affirmed that your body is inherently good, endowed with dignity and intended for God's glory. Jesus assumed a body and rescued us with it, and we look forward to the resurrection and glorification of our bodies in him. Our bodies can be sources of suffering, but they are not our adversaries. Our flesh, which is our capacity for sin and a source of sinful desires, is what we are called to crucify.

Some of the earliest heresies in the Church taught that the body was evil and that it had to be overcome or escaped. Modern culture treats the body as something we can change and overcome according to our will. It is important that we do not view our bodies and their needs and weaknesses as something to hate. Our bodies are gifts from God and temples of the Holy Spirit—worthy of respect, compassion, and love.

If the primary motivation for holiness is our vision of a holy God, then it follows that our secondary motivation is the understanding of who we are in him. The nature of Jesus, the Holy One who was obedient unto death, is now our true nature through the indwelling of the Holy Spirit. And so it follows that **holiness is our new normal**. A holy life should be natural, pleasing, and necessary to who we are. Sin is now unnatural, powerless, and unpleasant.

The evil desires that come from your flesh are not coming from you; in fact, they "wage war against your soul" (1 Peter 2:11). The life of the Spirit in you is your true self. If you can think this way about yourself, it will change how you relate to sin and how you understand righteousness and holiness. **Jesus did not redeem your flesh (your inclination toward sin). He unplugged you from it and plugged you into his grace.**

Imagine two of those inflatable lawn decorations (like Santa and his reindeer at Christmas), each one of them looking exactly like you. One is filled with air, vibrant and sturdy. The other is deflated—empty, lifeless, and limp. The first represents your nature in Christ, and the other, your flesh. You could pick up your deflated self and try to use it, but it is no longer alive. Your nature in Christ, animated by God's grace, is the real you.

Three Aspects of God's Grace

God's grace has three fundamental aspects. First, grace is *God's favor*, an expression of his love and pleasure. The angel Gabriel said to Mary, "Hail, full of grace, the Lord is with you!" (Luke 1:28). God's favor comes to us through Jesus. "From his [Jesus'] fulness have we all received, grace upon grace" (John 1:16). God's favor, which rested upon Jesus, now belongs to us, as we belong to him.

The words of the Father, "This is my beloved Son, with whom I am well pleased" (Matthew 3:17), express the truth about God's love for us. Jesus promised to make the Father known to us so that the Father's love would live within us (see John 17:26). The first characteristic of God's grace is God's love, which adopts us as his sons and daughters. By grace we share in the sonship of Jesus. When God looks at us, his heart is full of pleasure.

Second, grace is **_divine power_**. God gives us the inspiration and the power to walk away from sin and to walk in holiness. St. Paul writes, "God is at work in you, both to will and to work for his good pleasure" (Philippians 2:13). The apostle describes the cooperative way that God's power worked in his life: "[B]y the grace of God I am what I am, and his grace toward me was not in vain. On the contrary, I worked harder than any of them, though it was not I, but the grace of God which is with me" (1 Corinthians 15:10).

God's power equips us with everything we need for a holy life. When we work, God works with us and in us. Whatever God asks of us, he will empower us to do.

Third, grace is **_a share in God's own life_**. Grace is God living in you. St. Paul writes, "I give thanks to God always for you because of the grace of God which was given you in Christ Jesus, that in every way you were enriched in him" (1 Corinthians 1:4-5). The Father gives us his life in Jesus, whom we receive by the Holy Spirit. If God lives in you, then there is always a reason for hope, for nothing is impossible with God (see Luke 1:37). The truth of his grace, alive in you, means that the power of sin no longer reigns over or animates your life. Rather, God does.

Dying and Rising with Christ

Let's revisit what Jesus did on the cross. Jesus was our champion, contending on our behalf. When David stepped forward to fight Goliath, he did so as a champion. That meant that he fought on behalf of Israel, while Goliath fought on behalf of the Philistines. The fate of Israel rested upon David. If David lost the fight, then all of Israel would suffer the loss and become slaves of the Philistines. If David won, then Israel would share in the victory. In that moment, David was Israel, and Israel was in David. It is the same when we cheer on our favorite Olympic athletes from our country. We identify with them, they represent us, and their victory or defeat becomes ours. Our country competes in and through these individual champions.

In the same way, when Jesus suffered and died on the cross, he did it *as one of us*. The fate of our humanity rested upon Jesus. *Therefore, in him, every one of us can die and rise again in Baptism.* When you were baptized into Christ, you entered his death and resurrection. Jesus' passion did not just earn you an acquittal; it was your rebirth. Take the words of St. Paul as your own: "[I]t is no longer I who live, but Christ who lives in me; and the life I now live in the flesh I live by faith in the Son of God, who loved me and gave himself for me"(Galatians 2:20). Your flesh, which you might consider your "self," is dead. It died on the cross, along with you. Your life, as well as your true identity, is Christ living in you. That is who you really are.

Paul invites us to "live by faith in the Son of God" (Galatians 2:20). Do you trust enough in the nature of Jesus living within you to identify completely with him? Your life and your holiness flow from him. This is what is means to be "in Christ."

Being "in Christ" radically changes our attitudes toward sin. St. Paul teaches us,

> Do you not know that all of us who have been baptized into Christ Jesus were baptized into his death? We were buried therefore with him by baptism into death, so that as Christ was raised from the dead by the glory of the Father, we too might walk in newness of life. (Romans 6:3-4)

St. Paul is not saying that we can't sin, that we are unable to sin. He is saying that a lifestyle of sin is no longer an option for those whose life is in Christ, for in Christ there is no sin. Our new life has nothing to do with sin: "[O]ur former man was crucified with him so that the sinful body might be destroyed, and we might no longer be enslaved to sin. For he who has died is freed from sin" (Romans 6:6-7).

Our flesh, our old nature ruled by sin, has died. Therefore our new nature in Christ is free from sin's power. This is amazing news! Now Paul brings us a clear vision about how we should relate to sin:

> So you also must consider yourselves dead to sin and alive to God in Christ Jesus.
>
> Let not sin therefore reign in your mortal bodies, to make you obey their passions. Do not yield your members to sin as instruments of wickedness, but yield yourselves to God as men

who have been brought from death to life, and your members to God as instruments of righteousness. For sin will have no dominion over you, since you are not under law but under grace. (Romans 6:11-14)

Consider yourself dead to sin and alive to God. That is the prerequisite attitude for a holy lifestyle. When you sin, don't consider it part of your identity or something that's natural for you. Consider yourself dead to it. From this perspective we can see our choices as opportunities to live as the new creation we have received.

A Shift in Perspective

One of my professors was a reconnaissance pilot in the British Royal Air Force during World War II. The casualty rate among these pilots was high; every flight carried with it the terror of impending death. The professor said that for the first few months, death seemed to be around every turn. He was debilitated by the fear of it.

After those first few months, my airman professor considered the worst possible outcome: his death. He chose to embrace it and no longer fight to avoid it. He considered himself already dead. If the worst had already happened, then he no longer needed to be afraid.

My professor sensed a shift in his attitude. Now he could do his job with a sense of serenity and even joy. What changed? His perspective.

It is the same with our relationship to sin. When we identify with sin, we are terrified that it is really our nature, that we belong to it. This fear is described by Aleksandr Solzhenitsyn: "The line dividing good and evil cuts through the heart of every human being. And who is willing to destroy a piece of his own heart?"[20]

We might wrestle with our flesh, thinking we must change or perfect it. Instead, we need to consider ourselves dead to it. The worst (the best, really) has already happened: our old self was crucified with Jesus on the cross. The power of sin was broken, and we no longer belong to it.

Yet sin happens. What if the next time you sin, instead of beating yourself up or making judgments about who you are, you say, "That's not me. I'm dead to that. I don't need this in my life because I am alive in Christ."

Recently, at a retreat, I encouraged all the participants to pen a "breakup letter" with their flesh. The goal of the exercise was to help them recognize their flesh as something that no longer belonged to them. The results were hilarious. One began, "Dear sinful nature, I have found someone new, and he makes me truly happy. His name is Jesus, and he loves me in ways you never could."

One young man put his words to rap and performed for everyone. The atmosphere in the room became light and joyful as people gave expression to this "breakup" with their old self.

St. Ambrose recalls the story of a young man who was approached by an old flame with whom he had had a sinful relationship. He appeared to not recognize her, and she said, "It is I." He replied, "But I am not the former I."[21] Knowing that he was a new creation meant that he no longer had to wrestle with his past sins. Sin had happened, he had done it, but it was no longer his. He was not a slave to his past.

Out for a run one day, I started thinking about a persistent sin in my life. It was unpleasant to think about the many times I had failed in this area. Then I had an epiphany: Jesus had already overcome my sin. Even though I hadn't experienced the victory, it was a done deal. One day I would no longer wrestle with this sin. I could rejoice in what Jesus did to set me free.

I felt an exhilarating joy throughout my body, and I began to praise God for his victory. I felt like leaping and dancing for joy. It was as if my heart were transported to the finish line, even as I was in the middle of a race. This is the hope that Jesus brings.

Hope is a confident expectation for good, and it is rooted in what Jesus has done for us. He gives us his victory, one that we will one day see in its ultimate fulfillment. His grace will have its way in the end, and we can trust that "where sin increased, grace abounded all the more" (Romans 5:20). Corrie ten Boom recorded her sister's words from Ravensbrück, a German concentration camp: "There is no pit so deep that He is not deeper still."[22]

Go for It!

If sin does not define our identity, then we don't have to be afraid. We can be as violent as we need to be with evil desires when they arise. St. Paul uses violent words to describe how we can relate to sin: "crucify" the desires of the flesh; "take no part in" the deeds of darkness; "put off" your former way of life (see Galatians 5:24; Ephesians 5:11; 4:22). It's as if he is saying, "Go for it! Get rid of all of it!"

Don't hesitate to get rid of something that no longer serves you. "For just as you once yielded your members to impurity and to greater and greater iniquity, so now yield your members to righteousness for sanctification" (Romans 6:19). Holiness means taking all the energy that you used to spend trying to gratify your flesh and spending it instead on the righteousness that lives in you through Christ.

I know several people whose conversion brought them out of addiction and a truly evil lifestyle. It amazes me how these people are so passionate and energetic about sharing their faith, praising God, and doing good deeds. They use the same "hustle" they used to seek pleasure and direct it toward their new lives. Instead of the emptiness that came from trying to satisfy the flesh, they pursue joy. They have learned to starve their flesh and feed their spirit.

Let us not allow the things that are passing away to distract us from what is our life and destiny. St. Paul tells us:

> Therefore be imitators of God, as beloved children. And walk in love, as Christ loved us and gave himself up for us, a fragrant offering and sacrifice to God.
>
> But immorality and all impurity or covetousness must not even be named among you, as is fitting among saints. (Ephesians 5:1-3)

Not only are we dead to sin, but it isn't a good fit for us anymore. Sin is improper for our redeemed nature. What is the new normal? A life of sacrificial love that looks like Christ. We are holy children who resemble our loving Father, holy people doing what holy *is*. St. Peter tells us to "like living stones be yourselves built into a spiritual house, to be a holy priesthood, to offer spiritual sacrifices acceptable to God through Jesus Christ" (1 Peter 2:5).

Our life is now, like Jesus', both sacrificial and pleasing to God. We are holy, and we belong to God's family. As priests, we are called to worship at his throne and give him glory.

And the good news doesn't stop there. We are not only priests but also God's children. St. Paul writes,

> [F]or once you were darkness, but now you are light in the Lord; walk as children of light (for the fruit of light is found in all that is good and right and true), and try to learn what is pleasing to the Lord. Take no part in the unfruitful works of darkness, but instead expose them. (Ephesians 5:8-11)

Children learn from their parents, who model for them how to live. Through our relationship with the Father, we can discover the depths of goodness, righteousness, and truth. It is a learning process by which we live out who we are.

Finally, remember that Jesus made us holy because he loves us. "Christ loved the church and gave himself up for her, that he might sanctify her" (Ephesians 5:25-26). The source of our being holy is the love of God.

Therefore, the essential expression of our holiness is to love others just as he does. When we love the people around us in a sacrificial and life-giving way, we consecrate them to him and make the earth an altar.

Prayer

Father, thank you for the gift of grace. Thank you for my new nature in Christ, a nature that is no longer ruled by sin. Thank you for rescuing me from my flesh and for the life of Jesus within me. He is my life now, and I have died to sin.

Please reveal to me my true identity and help me live in it. I leave my shame behind, at the cross. And I offer myself to you as a holy living sacrifice.

REFLECTION QUESTIONS
(For Individual Use or with a Small Group)

1. Do you identify more with your new nature in Christ or with your old sinful nature? Do you see yourself as a saint who wrestles with sin or as a sinner who is trying to become holy?

2. How does shame hinder us from the pursuit of holiness? How might you address the role that shame plays in your life?

3. What is grace? How can you practice depending on and living by God's grace?

4. Write a "breakup letter" to your flesh, as if you were leaving a bad relationship. Explain why you no longer identify with your flesh. Describe the new life you enjoy.

CHAPTER 5

What Holiness "Does"

As He died to make men holy,
Let us die to make men free.
                              —The Battle Hymn of the Republic

U p until now, I have primarily focused on what it means to be holy. I have emphasized that we are made holy by the blood of Jesus—by his grace, his Spirit, his life in us. However, the fact that we are holy does not mean that we are *walking in holiness*. To walk in holiness is to align our wills with God's will and, in the process, become radically available to God.

That might sound like nice pious language fit for a holy card or a spiritual meme on social media. But walking in holiness involves the concrete, practical choices we make in our everyday lives. This is the territory of the Incarnation. Walking in holiness is not theoretical; it is real.

In Jesus' life and death, his every action, gesture, and word reveal what radical availability to God looks like. Through

Jesus' passion, death, resurrection, and ascension, he makes it possible for us to live out that lifestyle of availability.

Avoiding Unholy Pride and Shame

For many of the people I have met through Heart of the Father Ministries—those I have prayed with, listened to, formed, or served—holiness remains a mystery. "Is it even possible for me to live a holy life?" and "What does that really look like?" are questions often burning in their hearts.

You might think it only natural, then, that I started this book describing what walking in holiness looks like. However, the enemy hates the children of God. Through lies, accusation, and temptation, he seeks to guide the sons and daughters of God down a false path of either unholy pride or shame.

Unholy pride seeks to overcome insecurity by performing righteous acts, often for the approval of others. This kind of pride can lead to legalistic approaches to a relationship with God, comparing ourselves with others and placing our confidence in ourselves instead of the grace of God. I covered some of these approaches in chapter 2.

Shame drives us away from God, prompting us to hide or distance ourselves from him. We seek a place of punishment that we think we deserve. Shame can lead to false humility, timid living, and inferiority. Shame causes us to bury our talents and place limits on our lives or our thoughts of the future. I shared about the problem of shame and how we can overcome it in chapter 4.

I waited until now to explore walking in holiness so that we could first build a foundation in our understanding of holiness. At the root is the truth that we don't pursue holiness to *become holy* but rather pursue holiness because we *are holy*. Knowing that we are holy, as well as knowing that this is not the result of our performance but due to the merits and grace of Jesus Christ, is the antidote to both unholy pride and shame. The blood of Jesus has sanctified us, and there is nothing we can add to his sacrifice that will make us holy.

Pride has no place here. Christ has made us holy, and God will not stop loving us because of our failures. We don't need to hide in shame either. What we are is because of the grace of God. What we will be, including the holiness produced in our lives, is also the result of his grace working in us. Neither pride nor shame can change that. To embrace a holy lifestyle, we need to leave these two behind.

Why Does Living in Holiness Matter?

If the righteousness of Christ lives in me, then why does it matter how I live? There are two reasons, at least.

First, as mentioned before, holiness enables us to see God more clearly. Second, God didn't make you holy with only you in mind. The light God has placed in your life has a purpose: to serve others. The righteousness of Jesus within you can be displayed or obscured by your way of life.

Think of a megawatt flashlight, with power to shine brightly over a long distance in many directions. Now imagine the

"

The ability of others to see

the goodness of God and

give him glory depends on

the light that we allow to

shine through us.

flashlight lens covered in grease and dirt. The light will not be as visible to others.

The lens through which God's glory is displayed in your life is your words and actions. Jesus said, "Let your light so shine before men, that they may see your good works and give glory to your Father who is in heaven" (Matthew 5:16). The ability of others to see the goodness of God and give him glory depends on the light that we allow to shine through us. St. Paul described the purpose of his life in this way: "[W]e who first hoped in Christ have been destined and appointed to live for the praise of his glory" (Ephesians 1:12).

Why do we live? What is our purpose in this life? Why should we pursue holiness?

We, too, have been chosen and marked for the praise of God's glory. In success or failure, victory or defeat, our holy lives can bring glory to God. Others can see the light of God's glory in us and believe.

God's purpose for the apostle Paul was that the Ephesians would believe because of his testimony about Jesus, which could be clearly seen in the way he lived. In turn, the lives of the believers in Ephesus would open the eyes of others to God's glory, and so on. We also have received the light of God's glory through the testimony of others. That is why holiness matters so much in this world.

I think about all the people I have known whose words and actions enabled me to see the goodness of God. I think first of my parents, who worked tirelessly to build a Christian community through deeply committed relationships, prayer, and service. I think of my youth leaders, Ben and Kim, who allowed their hearts to break for me and my high school classmates. They always made space for me and invested time and love to share Jesus with me. They showed me how to love without conditions.

I think now of my friend Dave, who puts his wife first and loves her consistently. I think of my friend Tom, who always encourages me and shows me how to choose joy. And I think of my wife, Jenn, who loves people in all the hard and practical ways, always showing up when people are in need.

Every one of these people has shown me a different version of holiness. Their lifestyles have made an imprint on me, and my vision of God has expanded because of their witness to Christ. "For we are his workmanship, created in Christ Jesus for good works" (Ephesians 2:10).

You are a new creation, a beautiful work of God. You are a masterpiece! However, you are not some trophy or a ship in a bottle. You don't passively display God's glory. You are a working piece of beauty and brilliance, and the nature of Jesus is revealed in your humanity—how you live, love, speak, and serve.

Holiness involves intentionality, learning, decisions, actions, and the development of habits. Holiness is the road we walk when we decide to follow Jesus by loving God with all our hearts, souls, minds, and strength.

You might ask, "If I'm holy, shouldn't holiness just come to me naturally?" Not really.

Most of us learned another way of life before we encountered Jesus or surrendered our hearts to him. We might have spent years being discipled by the world, the flesh, and the devil. Even those of us raised as followers of Jesus have been affected by original sin and the world we live in. There is a lot that we must unlearn and a whole new way of life to discover.

Discovering and practicing what Christ has put inside of you can take time and effort. Imagine that a package arrived at your door, and inside it was a red cape with a bright yellow "S" on it. If you had never read a Superman comic book, you would have no idea what it was for. You might try it on as a nice-looking accessory.

But Superman has actually given you his superpowers! As you go through your day wearing his cape, you discover that you have x-ray vision, you can fly, and you are faster than a locomotive! Only by practicing Superman's lifestyle will you discover what is possible.

Our life in Christ is similar. There are powerful gifts inside us, good works planned for us, and spiritual fruit beginning to blossom because we have the Spirit of Jesus inside us. However, these will not be unveiled without our cooperation. You will only discover some of God's gifts as you use them.

Discipleship

Discipleship is an educational relationship in which a student learns to live as his teacher does. In ancient Greece, *paideia* was a model of education that prepared young aristocrats to be well-rounded citizens capable of leading a city. The curriculum was not a series of books or topics; the program wasn't simply about mastering content. Rather, it was an apprenticing relationship with a teacher who imparted a lifestyle to the student. In many cases, the students lived with their tutors so that they could learn by imitation.

Jewish rabbis and other religious leaders, including Jesus, taught their students in the same way. Disciples did not just show up for class; they followed their teachers and lived with them to learn their way of life. They did not study methods; they sat at the feet of a master.

Perhaps this story will make things even clearer: A father was teaching his son how to play basketball, and one day he turned on the television to show his son a master at work. "Don't watch any of the other players," the father said. "Just keep your eyes on number 3" (who was the great point guard Allen Iverson). The father instructed the boy to watch how the master played with the ball, how he played without the ball, and how he played defense. With a laserlike focus on the details of every move Iverson made, the boy began to learn from the best.

True discipleship is spending time with Jesus and watching his every move. If I want to grow in holiness, then Jesus is my model for life, for he is the holy God who lived a holy human life. And now he lives in me by faith and the sacramental life of the Church. I want to imitate his lifestyle so that, through God's grace, I can become more like him. This is the first stage of discipleship.

Imitation

What does imitating Jesus look like? Jesus gave his disciples many instructions and demonstrations. Then he sent them out to preach and do what they had seen him do. So we begin by observing Jesus and then attempting to do as he did.

Imitating Jesus may seem awkward at first. It will stretch us beyond our comfort zone, as it did the disciples. It might also involve some failures. The disciples would return to Jesus after attempting to imitate him, and Jesus would instruct them about what they were missing (see Matthew 17:14-21; Mark 9:17-29).

We need to keep looking to Jesus as our model. The most basic definition of discipleship that I know is this: "Monkey see, monkey do." Whatever I see in Jesus, I seek to put into practice in my life. Whatever sin is in me, I seek to put out of my life.

I expect the steps to maturity to be necessarily immature. However, as I set Jesus in my sights, I trust that he will guide my steps. As the Book of Proverbs says,

> Trust in the LORD with all your heart,
>   and do not rely on your own insight.
> In all your ways acknowledge him,
>   and he will make straight your paths. (3:5-6)

It's important to note here that simple imitation of Jesus, without a personal relationship that allows us to cooperate with the grace he died to give us, will not yield the fruits of holiness. This isn't about our effort; we cannot "imitate our way" to holiness. The *trust* that Proverbs talks about includes a decisive and constantly deepening surrender to the Lord. We recognize our inability to save ourselves and intentionally cooperate with his power and presence within us.

Imitation will only get us so far. Watching film of Allen Iverson and trying to mimic his moves: these alone will not make you a great basketball player. There are fundamental skills, habits, and principles that must be learned.

Understanding

The second stage of discipleship is understanding. I need to develop the *mind of Christ*. I need to see the world the way he sees it. I want to incorporate into my life his values, his priorities, and the motives by which he operates. As Paul writes, "Do not be conformed to this world but be transformed by the renewal of your mind, that you may prove what is the will of God" (Romans 12:2).

What is God's perspective on my relationships, my work, and my life? What is important to Jesus that should also be important to me?

Jesus taught his disciples about prayer, fasting, forgiveness, acting justly—and, most importantly, the kingdom of God. Many times Jesus provided his disciples with an "attitude adjustment." For example, in Luke 9, the people of a Samaritan village did not welcome Jesus because he was heading for Jerusalem. James and John asked Jesus if he wanted them to call down fire upon the village. Jesus "turned and rebuked them," and some ancient authorities would add Jesus' words, "You do not know what manner of spirit you are of!" (9:55).

The disciples were caught up in the ethnic prejudices of Jews and Samaritans. They couldn't see that God wanted to redeem the Samaritans, not burn them. Their attitude was more aligned with the devil's kingdom than with God's.

I remember a time when God shared with me his perspective and his values in a jarring way. I was attending an early morning Mass with many bleary-eyed men whose voices were not destined for the opera. Our attempt to sing "Let There Be Peace on Earth" was more like croaking than singing! When we got to the line "Let me walk with my brother, in perfect harmony," we all started to laugh. Even the deacon and priest could not keep a straight face!

In that moment of levity and laughter, I heard the Lord speak to my spirit with a stern warning: "Don't *ever* judge my children for how they worship me." Jesus was sharing with me his value for the worship that his people bring. It is precious to him. Even if our voices don't harmonize, God is thrilled when we turn our hearts to him.

I'll never forget that moment. I especially remember it when I'm tempted to be distracted by someone's voice, a bad sound system, or poor instrumentation. The Lord wasn't just modeling a behavior for me to imitate; he was unveiling his heart and inviting me to share in his point of view.

One of the best places to begin meditating on Jesus' ways is the Sermon on the Mount (see Matthew 5–7). In these teachings, Jesus reveals to us a lifestyle and mindset that fully embrace God's kingdom. He gives us *understanding*—principles of mercy, justice, kindness, and compassion. When we make these values our own, we will know when and how to apply them. Then our discipleship becomes not just a matter of imitation but also one of representing God's kingdom through our lifestyle.

Again, putting on the mind of Christ is not something that we can merely *will* to make happen. As we meditate on the principles of God's kingdom, the Holy Spirit, in union with Jesus, leads us to an understanding that is more than intellectual. The Spirit reveals to us the hidden things of God. We see this in Paul's writing to the church at Corinth: "Now we have received not the spirit of the world, but the Spirit which is from God, that we might understand the gifts bestowed on us by God" (1 Corinthians 2:12).

What the Spirit reveals to us, he enables us to receive. As we, through God's grace, put on the mind of Christ, we truly see the world with new eyes. We will explore this more in the section of this chapter on sanctification.

Practice (Just Do It!)

The third stage of discipleship is practice. You can study Jesus' teachings on forgiveness for many years; *doing* what you have learned is a whole different story. Practice is habitually doing things that strengthen our souls. Paul tells Timothy, "Train yourself in godliness" (1 Timothy 4:7). That means we should do things that strengthen our ability to live like Jesus in the real world.

Anyone can pray on occasion, forgive at times, or exercise generosity when their hearts move them. However, can we do these things when we don't feel like it? Fasting, prayer, giving, and serving are not just for when we feel like it. They are training exercises that strengthen our minds, wills, and emotions for the trials, temptations, and opportunities that life will bring.

In the Garden of Gethsemane, Jesus warned his disciples to keep watch and pray, "that you may not enter into temptation" (Matthew 26:41). Even though the disciples failed the test in the garden, Jesus was teaching them to train themselves for the challenges ahead. St. Paul writes in Ephesians 6 about how to take up the "armor of God"—truth, righteousness, the gospel, faith, salvation, God's word, prayer—to protect ourselves against the attacks of the enemy. All this so that "having done all, [we are able] to stand" (6:13; see 6:14-18).

Practice involves things that we do *before* the trials and temptations, things that prepare us for the test. Practice growing in your faith *before* it is challenged. Practice sharing the gospel *before* you have an opportunity to share it. Practice reading and meditating on Scripture *before* you need to apply it. Then, when the storm comes, you will be able to make your stand.

As a young man, I worked during the summers as a landscaper for the local school district. It wasn't the best job for me since I was allergic to spring grasses and sneezed nonstop! Plus it was a dirty, boring job, one that made me grateful for the privilege of a college education and the opportunities that I had before me.

I worked alongside a crew of full-time employees. Many of these men were hardened by a life full of mistakes, resentments, and regrets. I knew that they had only their weekends and retirement to look forward to. Much of their days were spent watching the clock and waiting to go home. I wanted to be a witness to God's love for them, and my lifestyle stood out like a sore thumb. I prayed and read the Bible during my lunch break. I didn't engage in lewd conversations or ogle women when they walked by. The men teased me relentlessly for not taking advantage of the opportunities of being young and unmarried.

Most importantly, however, I worked very hard. I gave my very best to a job that to many would seem meaningless. I tried to always show respect for the other men and the work they did all year.

On the first night of one summer's work, I had a "God dream." I don't know how to explain it, but in some of my dreams, I just know God is present and speaking to me, even if I don't understand what he is showing me. Very clearly in this dream, I heard God say, "His name is Edward."

Now, the driver of our landscaping crew and second in command was a guy named Eddie. So I sensed that God had given me an assignment. I prayed for Eddie throughout the summer. I prayed that God would touch his heart and that Eddie would know God's love for him.

On my very last day at the job, Eddie pulled me aside. "I know that you believe in God. I want you to know why I don't," he said. He proceeded to tell me about a girlfriend he had in high school and how much he had loved her. After his senior year, he was driving drunk and got into an accident, killing his girlfriend. "I can't believe in God because I'm angry. I don't know why he took her and didn't take me!" he cried.

In that moment, I knew exactly why God had placed me in that job. I took time to listen to Eddie and to feel his loss. I shared with him about God's love and mercy. I let him know that perhaps God wanted him to let go of his anger toward himself and God.

Eddie didn't express faith that day, but I know that he was able to share his burden with me and that a door of hope was opened. As I left work that day, I felt a profound sense of gratitude. My entire summer was spent with a weed eater in my hands and a purpose in my heart. That summer prepared me to share God's love with one person in one single afternoon. It was entirely worth it.

The practices of that summer—working hard, reading, praying, receiving insults without responding, being patient, and remaining innocent—were forming my character. They also presented a consistent message to the men around me, witnessing to them that God is real and that faith is possible. For Eddie it meant that he could open his heart to me and trust me with the source of his pain. That was a holy moment for which God had prepared me.

I have often heard the phrase "Practice random acts of kindness and senseless acts of beauty." It is a lovely thought to go through life doing creatively kind and beautiful things. However, for a disciple of Jesus, acts of kindness should not be random; rather, they should be intentional and consistent. It is through practice that acts of kindness become a regular expression of who we are in Christ.

In the Acts of the Apostles, an angel appears to the centurion Cornelius and tells him, "Your prayers and your alms have ascended as a memorial before God" (10:4). In response, God sends Peter to Cornelius' house so that all there can receive the gospel and the Holy Spirit. Like a fragrant incense, Cornelius'

"

If God is full of kindness and he lives in you, then you, too, can be full of loving kindness. If he is rich in mercy, then we are, too, for we are his children.

faithful and consistent practice of generosity and prayer had pleased God.

Discipleship in Action

When we incorporate imitation, understanding, and practice, the result will be a lifestyle that reflects the nature of Jesus in us. Let's look at an example.

Say you want to demonstrate the kindness of Jesus in your life. Start by imitating him. What did Jesus do that was kind? You could meditate on the kindness he showed the woman caught in adultery or on his words to the thief on the cross. You might notice how often he allowed individual people to have his complete attention, despite the crowds that surrounded him. How did Jesus respond with kindness in different situations? How might you imitate his words and actions?

Try stopping what you are doing when a person approaches you. Give the person your complete respect and full attention. Listen carefully to their needs, and speak to them with an awareness of God's love for them.

After imitating Jesus, seek to understand his ways. In Scripture you will discover that the kindness of God leads us to repentance (see Romans 2:4), that his kindness and mercy saved us (see Titus 3:4-5), that the Father is rich in mercy and full of loving kindness (see Ephesians 2:4-7). What does that mean for you?

If God is full of kindness and he lives in you, then you, too, can be full of loving kindness. How wonderful are his ways! If he is rich in mercy, then we are, too, for we are his children.

Finally, find opportunities to practice. Consecrate your hands to God for demonstrations of his kindness. Renounce violence in all its forms. Practice meditation and silence so that you may walk in the peace of God. Carefully measure your thoughts, according to the knowledge of God, before you speak.

As you seek to imitate Christ, know his ways, and put them into practice, the grace of God will enable you to demonstrate his kindness. Consider how you might show kindness with your eyes, with your arms, with your voice, with your resources, and with your time.

Sanctification

While you walk the path of discipleship, God is engaged in another process inside you: he is pouring out his grace to help you grow in holiness. The Church calls this sanctification.

Sanctification is the interior work of God's grace that brings freedom from sin, union with God, and an increasing love for God and others. This process integrates and works in (and through) the journey of discipleship. It is not magic, however. Sanctification requires our assent and continuous cooperation.

As a child grows, she needs help from her parents—a lot of help at first and less as she matures. Wise parents allow their child to struggle, without help at times, in order to learn.

God the Father will empower you for a life of holiness, but he will not take away your freedom. How much help will he give? Scripture is clear: "His divine power has granted to us all things that pertain to life and godliness" (2 Peter 1:3).

Below are two lists based on Scripture describing what God will and will not do for you.

What God will do:	What he will not do:
Fill you with his love.	Force you to love others. (Romans 5:5)
Give you wisdom and revelation.	Make you praise him. (Ephesians 1:17)
Convict you of sin.	Force you to repent. (John 16:8)
Give you spiritual gifts.	Make you use them. (2 Timothy 1:6)
Give you the desire to do his will.	Do it for you. (Philippians 2:13)
Prepare works in advance for you to do.	Make you do them. (Ephesians 2:10)
Give you hope and purify your heart.	Purify your lifestyle. (James 4:8; 1 John 3:3)

We can trust God to empower us in every way that does not take away our ability to choose. If we are intentional about cooperating with the grace that God gives us, he will give us more.

We get stuck when we resist the grace that God gives us. It is good to ask God if there is an area of your heart that needs repentance so that you can say yes to what he is empowering you to do. Sometimes God seems to be silent, but often his silence simply emphasizes the last thing he told you to do that you haven't done yet!

We also should pay attention to what God is empowering during different seasons of life. In some seasons, you will experience an increase of faith, generosity, humility, or compassion. When you become aware of an increase of God's grace or divine empowerment in an area of your life, it is time to let out your sails. Focus on what God is empowering, and aim to do it to a greater degree so that you can take hold of what he is giving you. Faithful stewardship in God's kingdom will lead to greater responsibility and authority.

There was a season of my life in college when I was intensely focused on learning how to hear God's voice. I would daily ask God to speak to my heart and give me the grace to obey. One day I felt that the Spirit was asking me to go sit down on a bench outside the math building. At the time, I had been placed in a very difficult math class where I did not belong, and I was preparing to drop the class. My average grade was a 16 percent!

I sat next to a young woman, and I said to her, "Hi, my name is Matt. I am a Christian, and I'm learning how to listen to God. I felt that God wanted me to sit down right here next to you. Is there anything I can do for you?"

Tears began flowing from her eyes. "I'm so scared," she said. "I'm failing my math class, and I don't know what to do about it. I've never failed a class before, and I don't know how I'm going to tell my parents."

I knew that God wanted me to encourage her, and so I did. I told her about my struggles with math, which cheered her up a bit. Then I prayed for her, that God would give her the grace to tell her parents and seek the help that she needed. She felt peace, and she began to smile. She told me that she was just praying for help when I walked up and sat down next to her! God had answered her prayer through my simple obedience.

Over the years, through experiences like this one, I have learned how to listen to and obey the promptings of the Holy Spirit. Small, seemingly foolish acts of obedience have helped me find greater intimacy with God. I have become more familiar with his voice. When we lean into his grace, we experience his power.

Faithfulness in small things prepares us for greater things. Jesus taught through his parables that his kingdom increases through faithful stewardship. Those who take care of what God entrusts to them will be given more.

Prayer

Lord, I want my lifestyle to display your glory. I want my words and actions to honor you and cause others to see you and give you praise. Help me cooperate with the grace that you have given me. Teach me your ways, and guide me as I follow you. Show me how I might put your words into practice during the day. Jesus, I trust you to sanctify my life.

REFLECTION QUESTIONS
(For Individual Use or with a Small Group)

1. Why does a lifestyle of holiness matter, to you and to God?

2. What did Jesus do that you want to imitate?

3. What values do you have because of your relationship with Jesus?

4. Write down some practices that you want to engage in to help you consistently live as Jesus did.

CHAPTER 6

Exploring a Lifestyle of Holiness

But thanks be to God, who in Christ always leads us in triumph, and through us spreads the fragrance of the knowledge of him everywhere. For we are the aroma of Christ to God.

—2 Corinthians 2:14-15

What are the basic ingredients of a holy lifestyle? I suggest three: purity, devotion, and integrity. All three of these are representations of the wholeness that Christ brings to our humanity. As we seek to make our lives more available to God, these elements will develop in us.

Purity

Purity often gets a bad rap, especially when it is presented solely in the negative—as in abstinence, colorlessness, or an empty joylessness. However, anyone in the food, beverage, or medicine industries knows that "purity" is a powerful word. Purity is the freedom from that which dilutes or corrupts the whole.

For example, have you ever been to Italy and tasted authentic Parmigiano Reggiano from Parma or balsamic vinegar from Modena? The moment you taste them, you know that "purity" means authenticity through and through, with no fillers or contaminants. Purity is potency. I tasted a pineapple in Tanzania from a roadside farm, fresh cut from the tree, and questioned whether I had ever had a real pineapple before.

For a Christ bearer, purity is the freedom from any expression of compromise, dilution, or hypocrisy that does not reflect the life of Jesus in all its potency. St. Paul says that "immorality and all impurity or covetousness must not even be named among you, as is fitting among saints" (Ephesians 5:3). Are there things in your life that dilute the image of Christ in you?

Just like those who produce fine foods and beverages, Christians must have a relentless passion for purity. If the product isn't pure, the producer starts over.

Many of us would rather level off on purity when it is comfortable. "I want to appear pure, but I can tolerate a little bit of immorality." Perhaps we piously attend Mass but interiorly bow to idols of greed and comfort. Many of us, if we are honest, prefer to leave that "hint" of something else in the mix.

"

Ask God for strategies

to help you walk in

greater purity. Ask for his

grace and love to fill you.

Since we have been redeemed by the love of Jesus, we can be ruthless toward our sins. As we mentioned earlier, Paul uses violent words like "crucify" and "put to death" to describe what to do with sinful desires (see Galatians 5:24; Colossians 3:5). Passion for Jesus consumes sinful desires, as a crucible melts metals and purifies them. The process is not always comfortable, but it is an expression of love.

I encourage you to be completely honest with yourself. Make an inventory of the hints and impurities in your life. Bring them to Jesus, and confess them. Make a plan for how you intend to get rid of them. Sometimes it will require you to take a different path, to sacrifice something, or to make changes to your schedule. Ask God for strategies to help you walk in greater purity. Ask for his grace and love to fill you.

A friend once shared with me how he overcame his struggle with pornography. For many years it was a source of addiction and spiritual bondage. The Lord delivered him from that slavery, but after walking in freedom for a time, he returned to his sin. He brought it before the Lord and asked him for help.

The Lord showed my friend a strategy. Instead of reading the newspaper first thing in the morning, as was his normal routine, he should begin the day reading the Scriptures. Starting each day with the word of God, he was able to break a pattern of consuming information, feeding his curiosity, and then later succumbing to temptation at the end of the day, when he was tired and his defenses were weak. This small change in his life reaped huge rewards. By starting his day feasting on God's word, he broke the pattern of behavior that led to sin.

I believe that God has not only grace for us but also strategies, if we will listen. Some of these strategies involve "avoiding the near occasion of sin," which is a tremendous part of wisdom. Many nutrition experts will tell you, for example, that victory over bad eating habits begins at the grocery store, not the fridge.

Other strategies might involve trying something that is awkward and new. God might ask you to respond differently than you usually do when one of your children pushes your buttons. He might show you a new spiritual practice that you won't be good at right away. The important thing is that we channel our passion into obedience. Take steps in the direction in which God leads you, and do it right away. The cry of a pure heart is "Here I am, Lord. I want to do your will."

Devotion

The second element of holiness is devotion. Like purity, devotion involves a lack of division, but this time within the heart. Devotion means that God comes first; he takes the highest place in our affections.

When you love God first, you are choosing the best for yourself. St. Augustine described devotion in this way: "My love is my weight. If I love things above myself, I will rise. If I love things below myself, I will fall."[23] Devotion means putting our loves in proper order, reserving our worship for God, who alone is worthy.

Throughout the Old Testament, you can see that the power of sin often caused the human heart to stray through idolatry, the worship of something other than God. Idolatry is still a problem today. There are many good things in life that we can become attached to in an unholy way. When we put people, possessions, popularity, and pleasure at the center of our hearts, we become divided. When we rend our hearts of attachments and center our affections on God, we begin to see and love things and people in their proper place.

One of the ways we do this is through renunciation. Renunciation is an act of the will by which we say, "I'm done with this. I make no place for this in my life." We can renounce our idols in the name of Jesus. We can say, "In the name of Jesus, I renounce the idol of comfort." "In the name of Jesus, I renounce the idol of success." "In the name of Jesus, I renounce the idol of popularity." The *Catechism* reads, "There is no holiness without renunciation and spiritual battle."[24]

Pope Francis reflected on the renunciations in our baptismal vows:

In the same measure with which I say "no" to the suggestions of the devil—the one who divides—I am able to say "yes" to God who calls me to conform to him in thoughts and deeds. . . . It is necessary to detach oneself from certain bonds in order to truly embrace others. . . . For this reason, the renunciation and the act of faith go together. It is necessary to burn some bridges, leaving them behind, in order to undertake the new Way which is Christ.[25]

As we pursue holiness, it is important to recognize that we have choices in life. There are many things that we can say yes to. Holiness is about choosing the very best, over and over again. It is saying yes to God in everything.

In order for us to say yes, there often needs to be a *no*. When I said yes to my wife Jennifer in a covenant of marriage, I also said no, "forsaking all others." In order to express covenant faithfulness to my beloved, I must renounce every other romantic possibility. If I did not promise exclusivity, I would not be saying yes at all.

In our relationship with God, there will be times when we need to say *no* to other things so that we can give God a greater yes. Renunciation is an act of passionate devotion, not a sterile denial of self.

That being said, holiness is not just about saying no. What we say yes to is even greater.

St. Paul urges the Romans to "cast off the works of darkness," the ways of the flesh, and "put on the Lord Jesus Christ" and his virtues (13:12, 14). He tells the Galatians to crucify the desires of the flesh (see 5:24) and tells Timothy to fan into flame the gifts of God (see 2 Timothy 1:6). The Letter to the Hebrews says that we should "lay aside" sin, which easily entangles us, and run the race before us (12:1).

In fact, what you put on is essential to overcoming what you have put off. Studies show that discarding the neurological connections that form a habit is impossible. In other words, you can't just erase a bad habit from your brain. The best way to break the power of an old habit is to form a new habit—one that has a stronger neural pathway![26]

So how do I put off the ways of the flesh? By putting on Christ. How do I throw off entangling sin? By running my race. Paul makes this connection clear: "I say, walk by the Spirit, and do not gratify the desires of the flesh" (Galatians 5:16).

I am not suggesting that the kingdom of God is just a series of habits. No, the kingdom of God is righteousness, joy, and peace that comes from the presence and reign of Jesus in our hearts. The fruit of his reign will be expressed in our lives by a habitual disposition to joy, peace, self-control, and many other virtues.

Integrity

The third element of a holy lifestyle is integrity. The power of the kingdom of God permeates every aspect of our lives—from the workplace to church to home. We act with consistency and in accord with the moral life proposed by Jesus and his Church, regardless of our environment. We don't bend to popular opinion if it contradicts the ways of God.

One of the largest obstacles to living with integrity is *fear of man*. If we fear men, we are tempted to shrink back when our convictions clash with social acceptance. Peter demonstrated that kind of fear in the Gospel accounts of Jesus' passion.

At the Last Supper, Peter made a passionate declaration that he would follow Jesus anywhere, even to death. Just hours later, he abandoned Jesus and denied knowing him three times, even calling curses upon himself. Peter's problem was not a lack of faith: he believed that Jesus was the Messiah. His problem was a lack of integrity. He chose to be one person with Jesus, loyal and devoted, and another in the public square.

St. Mark notes some telling details in his Gospel: "Peter had followed him at a distance, right into the courtyard of the high priest; and he was sitting with the guards, and warming himself at the fire" (14:54). Peter chose to follow Jesus "at a distance," when the eyes of the world were upon him. Peter warmed himself at the fire of social acceptance and tranquil anonymity. The result was two Peters, in conflict with one another. When Jesus locked eyes with Peter after his betrayal, the apostle became aware of his brokenness and wept. He realized that he had betrayed the Lord for something fickle and cheap.

Have you ever found yourself in this place, feeling broken by your divided loyalties and knowing that you have betrayed your true self? Have you had those moments of disappointment in finding that your character was not what you thought it was? Times of testing and trial often reveal the true condition of our hearts.

After Jesus rose from the dead, he lovingly restored Peter to a place of leadership and service. Later, on Pentecost, Peter received the power and presence of the Holy Spirit, resulting in a profound change. A new boldness emerged as he preached the good news to the crowd in Jerusalem.

In Acts 5, we see Peter and the apostles preaching in the same Temple courts where Jesus had preached. They were arrested and thrown in the public jail, perhaps the same cell where Jesus had awaited his trial. They stood before the same Sanhedrin who had condemned Jesus as worthy of death, surrounded by the same Temple guards with whom Peter had stood around a fire, trying to blend in. Peter knew that he faced the possibility of death, yet he boldly declared with the other apostles,

We must obey God rather than men. The God of our fathers raised Jesus whom you killed by hanging him on a tree. God exalted him at his right hand as Leader and Savior, to give repentance to Israel and forgiveness of sins. And we are witnesses to these things, and so is the Holy Spirit whom God has given to those who obey him. (5:29-32)

The Sanhedrin was furious and wanted to kill the apostles, but the intervention of a wise Pharisee named Gamaliel persuaded them to release the apostles. After being flogged and told not to speak in the name of Jesus, Peter and the apostles rejoiced "that they were counted worthy to suffer dishonor for the name" (Acts 5:41) They went right back into the Temple courts, proclaiming Jesus as the Messiah!

The loving mercy of Jesus and the transforming power of the Holy Spirit brought Peter to a place of integrity, where he could face the rejection of men and speak the truth in love. His journey to integrity was not over, for later St. Paul would confront him on his fear of men and his desire to please others. God continued to provide Peter with trials and discipline, mercy and power, to help him reconcile his divided heart and live with integrity.

God will do the same for us.

Prayer

Lord Jesus, I am sorry for the ways that I have allowed sin to reign in my life. Please forgive me for the things I have loved in a disordered way and for choosing to put you second. Lord, I desire to have an undivided heart and a life of integrity. I ask you to give me strategies and wisdom so that I might put off the ways of the flesh and embrace my life in you.

REFLECTION QUESTIONS
(For Individual Use or with a Small Group)

1. What are some "hints" of impurity in your lifestyle that you want to address?

2. Devotion means putting your loves in proper order. Make a list of the passions in your life, in order of importance to you. Are there any that you need to reject or reorder?

3. The best way to erase a bad habit is to replace it with a new one. What habits could you adopt to help you "put on the Lord Jesus Christ" (Romans 13:14) and "walk by the Spirit" (Galatians 5:16)?

4. Invite Jesus to love you in the places where you are insecure and likely to fear man. Let his mercy and love fill your heart.

CHAPTER 7

Overcoming Obstacles

Anyone who desires to grow in holiness will experience the frustration of "hitting the wall." After some initial progress, we get stuck in some area of life, repeating old patterns of behavior. Don't be discouraged. Believe it or not, God is working in our lives during these times to set us free.

I clearly remember a moment when God set me free from spiritual bondage that I had suffered for most of my life. What started as a simple conversation about whether I should buy a new house had turned into a fit of anger toward my dad. "I don't want your advice!" I yelled as I hung up the phone, shaking with anger.

My dad and I normally got along fine, and I usually listened to his advice. My outburst was so unexpected that it left me confused. In that moment I realized that something inside me just wasn't right.

I am the third of four boys. When I was growing up, I often saw things from a different perspective than my brothers did, and this often led to arguments with everyone in my family. I would remember in detail something I had read or heard, and my brothers would accuse me of exaggerating. They would tease me and say that I made everything up. Other times I would offer a creative thought to our conversations, while they preferred black-and-white answers. As a result, I often felt defensive around them, afraid to share my thoughts.

We had many family meetings and even family counseling sessions in which we sought to resolve our differences. Some of these meetings became heated, as I felt singled out as the "problem" that my family needed to solve. I would lash out or try to run away. During one confrontation, I jumped out of a first-story window to get away!

Over time I began to believe that I was so different that no one would ever understand me. Whenever I felt misunderstood, it was so painful that I felt as if a knife were being twisted in my side. I would exaggerate or lie to avoid having to explain myself. I would argue and justify things I did. I would put on a false self, pretending to be the kind of person whom people could understand—anything to avoid that helpless and painful feeling of being misunderstood.

After my conversion to Christ in high school, I experienced lots of wonderful changes. The Lord transformed me from a sad, depressed, and angry teenager to a happy, loving person. In college I eagerly dove into prayer, reading Scripture, and building lasting friendships with other Christians. After college, God used my relationship with my wife to bring me to deeper levels of freedom. In Jennifer I found a person who truly knows me and loves me for who I am.

Despite all this change in my life, something was still holding me back. Whenever I encountered a sharp disagreement or felt misunderstood, I would resort to self-justification and anger. The fear of being misunderstood followed me into every relationship, and every conflict brought back that pain in my heart. Ten years after my conversion to Christ, the Holy Spirit used that moment of conflict with my dad about buying a house to set me free.

As my dad shared his concerns, I interpreted his words as a lack of confidence in me. Once again I felt the deep pain of feeling misunderstood. After hanging up on my dad, I suddenly realized that I still had wounds that needed to heal. I called my dad back and apologized, and I asked him if we could pray together.

I went to my dad's house, and he asked me some questions about what it was like growing up in our family. I shared about those moments when I felt so different, so misunderstood, and so alone. He began to pray with me, leading me to repent of my own sinful responses and to forgive my family members for not showing me the love I needed and for not understanding me.

I began to renounce the lies the devil had used to keep me bound up. Finally I said, "In the name of Jesus, I renounce the lie that no one could ever understand me." Prior to that moment, I had believed that my problem was other people, and now I saw that was a lie. When I renounced that lie in Jesus' name, its power to torment me was broken. I heard the

"

God has turned my

struggle into a great

blessing. He can do

the same for you.

whisper of God in my heart, "Son, I have always known you. I have always understood you."

Since that time, my life has changed dramatically. I no longer experience the crippling fear of being misunderstood or the driving need to defend myself. When someone corrects me or doesn't understand my point of view, I don't feel as though my world is collapsing, nor do I feel the anguish I used to experience. I know that I can run to my heavenly Father and receive his love and understanding.

I am unlearning the habit of self-justification. I am recognizing my own weaknesses instead of accusing or mistrusting other people. I am also learning appropriate ways to express myself, instead of treating people like accusers.

St. Paul wrote, "For we are not contending against flesh and blood" (Ephesians 6:12). This verse has taken on a new reality for me, as I realize that people are not my enemies. Rather, the deceptions that try to isolate and torment me are my true enemies.

Looking back, I can see that the devil's plan was to keep me from knowing my true identity in Christ. Today I write books and regularly speak before large groups of people. Surprisingly, communicating with clarity has become one of my strongest gifts. All the devil's lies had been aimed at keeping me from offering myself and my gifts freely in love.

What the devil intended for my destruction, God has redeemed. He has turned my struggle into a great blessing. God can do the same for you.

The Enemy and His Lies

As you pursue holiness, it is important to know that you have an adversary. Jesus called him "the father of lies" (John 8:44). The devil is a "thief [who] comes only to steal and kill and destroy" (10:10). How does he do it? Primarily through deception.

If the devil can deceive us, then he can hold us in bondage to the power of his lie. St. Thomas Aquinas defined freedom as "the ability to know . . . and to love the good."[27] If we don't know the good (because of deception), we won't be free to choose it. If growing in holiness requires that we choose what is good, then it is essential that we break free from the influence of the evil one's lies.

Most believers fight their sins solely as a weakness in their will. They think that if they just try hard enough, they will overcome those sins. Exercising our will is important, but the battle for our minds is just as important. In my story, it was not enough to simply fight my desire to justify and explain myself. I needed to renounce the lie that held me in bondage—the lie that no one understood me—so that I could see the truth clearly.

St. Paul wrote, "Put on the whole armor of God, that you may be able to stand against the wiles of the devil" (Ephesians 6:11). You have an adversary who wants to destroy your life and your relationship with God. He plots and schemes various ways to do that. For example, the enemy had a strategy to keep me from healthy relationships and from offering my gifts to others.

God wants you to be aware of the devil's strategies and take your stand against them. Our Father has not left us powerless before the lies and machinations of the devil. That is why at every Baptism, everyone stands to make a profession of faith, which begins by renouncing "Satan, all his works, and all his empty promises." Embracing the truth that sets us free involves rejecting the devil (the personal power behind sin), his works (evil deeds), and his empty promises (lies).

Let us examine, then, some of the common lies of the enemy and how to renounce them.

"God is not good, and he cannot be trusted."
This lie is the beginning of all sin. It is the deception that the serpent used to entice Adam and Eve (see Genesis 3:1-4). St. Paul writes about humanity under the power of sin: that "although they knew God they did not honor him as God or give thanks to him, but they became futile in their thinking and their senseless minds were darkened" (Romans 1:21).

When our intellect cannot perceive God as he is, our imagination substitutes a deficient image of him. This blindness toward the truth of God's character can stem from a failure to acknowledge God or give God a proper place in our lives. Remember that in chapter 2, we saw that loving God leads to seeing him with the eyes of our hearts. The opposite is also true: refusing to love him leads to a darkness that keeps us from seeing him. Love begets love, and sinfulness begets darkness, which leads to more sin.

Often when I minister to someone, I discover that fear, mistrust, and insecurity in their relationship with God lie at the root of their bondage to certain sins. Here are some examples of ways I have led people to repent for their "futile thinking":

"Lord, please forgive me for believing that I love my child more than you do."
"Lord, please forgive me for judging you and thinking that you don't want good things for me."
"Lord, forgive me for thinking that you love others more than you love me."
"God, I'm sorry for not trusting that you have plans for my life."
"God, please forgive me for thinking that I know better than you."
"Lord, I'm sorry for believing that you don't love me and want to punish me."
"Lord, please forgive me for believing that I have to perform in order to be loved by you."

"Something else will satisfy me."

When our minds have been darkened, we try to fill the void with something that God created rather than with God's glory. The Bible refers to this as idolatry. Modern people don't bow to carved idols so much, but our hearts and imaginations are still captured by created things like money, sex, power, and popularity. I once heard idolatry simply defined as "anything you consult before you consult God."

Where do we look for strength and support in times of trouble? What have we put our hope in? If it isn't God, then it is probably an idol.

While all created things are good, they can poison our hearts if they are misused or become something we worship. An idol will always fail to provide what we ask of it. If we spend our lives acquiring idols, they will break our hearts.

In short, idolatry is the result of disordered love. Below are some renunciations of idols and attachments:

"In the name of Jesus, I renounce the idol of people-pleasing."
"In the name of Jesus, I renounce my attachment to wealth."
"In the name of Jesus, I renounce the idol of (food, sex, control, power, money, and so on)."
"In the name of Jesus, I renounce the idol of relationships."
"In the name of Jesus, I renounce the idols of pleasure and comfort."

"I am never safe."

Fear is another thief. It is a coercive deception, driving us to try and preserve that which we can never keep: our lives, our time, our resources, and our hearts. We spend our energy trying to save our lives, and the result is that we lose them.

Jesus described these fears as weeds that choke the word of God, preventing it from taking root and being fruitful (see Matthew 13:7, 22). Fear diminishes our trust in God and his promises. One pastor said, "Would you trust a friend who lied to you as often as your fears do?" It's a good question. Why do we tolerate fear when it lies to us so often?

Below are some common fears you can renounce in the name of Jesus:

Fear of the future	Fear of failure
Fear of loss	Fear of men/women
Fear of tragedy	Fear of judgment
Fear of death	Fear of condemnation
Fear of abandonment	Fear of being alone
Fear of humiliation	Fear of lack
Fear of rejection	Fear of making mistakes

"It is hopeless."

Another deception is despair. When we despair, we embrace hopelessness, self-condemnation, and self-hatred. We do not exercise our freedom because we believe that we are powerless. The darkened mind reasons without God or his perspective, and the result is helplessness.

St. Paul wrote that "hope does not disappoint us, because God's love has been poured into our hearts through the Holy Spirit who has been given to us" (Romans 5:5). God's love, made known in Jesus, fills our hearts and gives us hope, even in the direst circumstances. When we know that God is for us, we can face the challenges of our lives with confidence. We know that we can overcome, for nothing can "separate us from the love of God" (8:39).

Below are some expressions of hopelessness that we can and must renounce in the name of Jesus:

"I will never succeed."	"I can never live a holy life."
"I will never be loved."	"There is never enough."
Despair	"I will always come last."
Self-hatred	"I am not chosen/important."

Self-condemnation "I am worthless."
"I'm not good enough." "I don't have what it takes."
"I am not holy." "I don't matter."
A victim identity ("I am helpless.")

"I must protect myself."
Finally there are the responses we make to traumatic events. When we are wounded or frightened, we make decisions and commitments that we think will protect us. Some choose independence and pride; others choose avoidance and fear. Some seek shelter in resentments, bitterness, and revenge.

These responses keep us imprisoned. They prevent us from being vulnerable, from taking hope-filled risks, from letting go of our sin. They cause us to take on false identities, like the lie that we are victims or unlovable persons. They limit our choices and our opportunities.

Below are some responses that we can renounce and repent of.

Self-protection Avoidance
Pride Escape
Superiority Fantasy
Independence Perfectionism
Mistrust The idol of performance
Resentment Self-reliance
Bitterness Control
Revenge "I can never trust a
Hatred man/woman again."

Violence   "I have to do it by myself."
Numbness   "It is all up to me."

Some of you might be reading this and thinking, "Wow, those are a lot of deceptions!" You might feel overwhelmed if you realize that many of the deceptions and coercions listed above have been part of your thinking. Don't be discouraged; God wants to help you get free from them.

God has given us a strategy to overcome the lies of the enemy. St. Paul wrote, "Do not be conformed to this world but be transformed by the renewal of your mind, that you may prove what is the will of God, what is good and acceptable and perfect" (Romans 12:2). Moving from bondage to freedom begins with the renewal of our minds. Renewed in our thinking, we can see the truth and choose what is good.

The Five Keys to Freedom

Renewing the mind involves responding in faith to what God has revealed to us. I would like to share with you five responses that will help you cooperate with the Holy Spirit in the renewal of your mind. Those of us involved in Unbound ministry call them the "Five Keys" of Unbound ministry. We have helped thousands of people use these keys and experience the power of God setting them free. You can learn more about these in a book by my father, Neal Lozano: *Unbound: A Practical Guide to Deliverance* (Chosen Books, 2010).

The first key is *repentance and faith*. The Greek word for "repentance" is *metanoia*, which means "to go beyond the mind that you have." Put simply, repentance is a change of mind that leads to a changed life. Faith is our grace-filled response to God's revelation. Jesus put these two responses—faith and repentance—together when he proclaimed, "The kingdom of God is at hand; repent, and believe in the gospel" (Mark 1:15).

What do you need to change your mind about? What do you need to respond to?

The gospel.

The gospel is simply the good news about our salvation in Jesus Christ and an invitation to enter into the kingdom of God. If freedom is about perceiving and choosing the good, then the good news is the beginning of every good choice. When we change our minds and surrender to God's reign, we invite his transformative power into our lives.

This is not just a one-time decision but a lifestyle of turning and yielding to God's love and truth. Believing the good news that God has redeemed us through his Son changes everything. In the light of his love, we can begin to see clearly the deceptions that have held us in chains or the sinful responses to life that keep us stuck. Turning from sin and trusting in Christ's power opens our hearts to receive hope and awakens love.

How do we repent and express faith? Use the same words that you learned in kindergarten: "sorry," "please," and "thank you":

- Tell God that you are sorry for your sins, your selfishness, and the false ideas you have held onto about him.

- Ask him to transform your life. Ask for his forgiveness and his friendship. Surrender to Jesus, and ask him to be the Lord of your life.
- Thank Jesus for his mercy and love displayed on the cross. Thank him for every good work he has done in your life. Thank him for his love.

Embracing the gospel is the beginning of saying yes to every good thing.

The second key to freedom is *forgiveness*. Forgiveness is surrender to God's healing power by giving up our right to hold on to an offense. When we offer forgiveness, we apply the truth of the gospel to the painful experiences of life and choose to identify with Jesus. Forgiveness allows his mercy to flow through our hearts to the ones who have wounded us.

Because we have received God's mercy, we have also been empowered to forgive others. How do we do it?

You can simply say, out loud, "In the name of Jesus, I forgive," then say the person's name and what they did or did not do that hurt you. Be specific, and name the place of your pain. Trust in the mercy of God as you forgive. Choosing to trust in God's sufficient love as we forgive helps us break free from the bondage of resentment and bitterness.

The third key is *renunciation*, which I introduced in chapter 6. We can renounce every lie, idol, sin, and evil spirit that keep us from freely choosing what is good. Renunciation means "I'm done with that." When we do it in the name of Jesus, we do it with the power and authority of a child of God.

Renunciation cuts our connections with the kingdom of darkness and the sin that easily entangles us. You can say, "In the name of Jesus, I renounce . . . " and then specifically name the things that have held you back. For example, "In the name of Jesus, I renounce hatred." "In the name of Jesus, I renounce the idol of approval." "In the name of Jesus, I renounce the lie that I am unlovable." Renunciation is a "no" that enables our "yes" to God and his kingdom.

The fourth key is *authority*. Paul teaches that we should take our stand against the devil's schemes. We need to recognize that we have a real enemy who seeks to rob us of our freedom, our identity, and our dignity. Using our will to express the authority we have as children of God is another valuable expression of freedom. We are not the devil's subjects any longer. We do not need to submit to sin's reign.

We can say, "In the name of Jesus, I command every spirit I have renounced to leave me right now." Many people who have lived with the weight of spiritual bondage for most of their lives experience a tangible lifting of that weight after exercising their baptismal authority in Jesus' name. Others experience their spoken words as a powerful expression of their will against the kingdom of darkness.

In the movie *The Lord of the Rings: The Two Towers*, Sméagol faces the accusations and taunting of his evil alter ego, Gollum, who speaks to him from within. At first he cowers in fear and shame, trying not to hear Gollum's lies: "You don't have any friends. Nobody likes you." Gollum reminds Sméagol of his haunted past: "You are a liar and a thief. *Murderer*."

Fed up with Gollum's tormenting voice, Sméagol begins to take his stand: "Leave now, and never come back." "Leave now, and never come back." "LEAVE NOW, AND NEVER COME BACK!" At last the Gollum leaves. And Sméagol rejoices, "Sméagol is free!"[28]

Like Sméagol, we can take up our authority as children of God and tell our enemies to leave.

The fifth key is the *Father's blessing*. To speak the Father's blessing means to speak the thoughts of God into the heart of a person. Led by the Holy Spirit, who is the Spirit of Sonship, we can hear and speak words that reflect the Father's heart.

The blessing can be a Scripture passage, a meaningful touch, a reflection on your name, a statement of your identity in Christ, or an acknowledgment of the good things God sees in you. God's thoughts are a treasure, and they empower us to fulfill our purpose in life. You can ask someone you trust to pray for you and to speak the words that God the Father gives them as a blessing on your life. Or, you can ask God to speak a blessing into your heart. Ask him questions like, "God, what is something that you love about me? What is something I did today that brought you joy?"

You can also get to know God's heart by speaking blessings to others. This awareness of the Father's love, of our identity as his children and our belonging to him, is the essence of what it means to be free. Jesus said,

> Truly, . . . every one who commits sin is a slave to sin. The slave does not continue in the house for ever; the son continues for ever. So if the Son makes you free, you will be free indeed." (John 8:34-36)

Jesus set us free so that we could take our place as sons and daughters of the Father. We have a place at his side. Stepping into this reality enables us to perceive who we are and whose we are. Knowing that we are pleasing to God awakens our love, and when we choose in the light of his love, we are empowered by his grace. Holiness becomes not a burden of service but, rather, an adventure of love and self-giving. We give and receive, and we are drawn into deeper communion with God. The result is abundant, eternal life.

Final Encouragement

Old habits die hard, and new habits can be hard to form. Our best efforts can fall short, and sometimes it is a struggle to get up and try again. In these times, it is important to remember three things.

First, Jesus understands. He knows what it is like to face temptation in every way. He is able to empathize with our weakness (see Hebrews 4:15).

Second, God celebrates and rewards even the smallest steps we take toward him. If we fall a hundred times, he cheers for us every time we get back up. God does not focus on criticizing us or dwelling on our failures. Even the smallest act of devotion and love is precious to him, and he will not fail to recognize and reward it (see Mark 9:41). God is a good Father.

Third, our path of discipleship and sanctification is not about becoming worthy or performing to God's expectations. It is about following Jesus, desiring to be faithful because we love him, and trusting God to complete the good work he began in

"

Holiness becomes

not a burden of service,

but, rather, an adventure

of love and self-giving.

The result is abundant,

eternal life.

us (see Philippians 1:6). God will use our failures and our successes to draw our hearts closer to him. Don't aim for success or an ideal of what your life should look like. Make following Jesus your aim, and healing and freedom will follow.

The One Thing

As you grow in the knowledge of God, you will grow in freedom. Your desire for what is good in your life will grow as you experience this freedom.

I have little knowledge of fine wines. If you asked me to choose the best from a few bottles, I wouldn't have much chance of selecting it. However, if you taught me about the qualities of good wine and gave me many opportunities to taste different ones, my ability to know and choose the best would grow.

Each time you choose what is good, your desire to grow in holiness will deepen. Jesus told his disciples to "lay up for yourselves treasures in heaven" (Matthew 6:20) instead of storing up treasure on earth. Choosing to work for God's pleasure instead of a worldly reward is a sacrifice, for earthly rewards are immediate though fleeting. As you choose heaven over earth, your heart becomes more in tune with the values of heaven. "For where your treasure is, there will your heart be also" (6:21). Sacrifice, therefore, is an expression of the heart's deepest desire.

Have you ever seen an Olympian win a gold medal? Their joy is overwhelming. Their tears and big smiles attest to how much they have sacrificed in pursuit of that medal. The value you have for something can be seen in the sacrifices you make to obtain it.

Everyone makes sacrifices. As Bob Dylan sings, "You're gonna have to serve somebody." Everyone worships the thing that has captured their heart.

When Martha complained to Jesus that her sister was not helping her, Jesus responded,

> Martha, Martha, you are anxious and troubled about many things; one thing is needful. Mary has chosen the good portion, which shall not be taken away from her. (Luke 10:41-42)

Sitting at Jesus' feet and doing the work of hospitality were both good, but Mary's choice was better—more valuable and more necessary than having a good meal and a clean home. It can be helpful to stop and ask yourself, "Am I choosing the better part? In my use of time, resources, and attention, am I spending my life on what is necessary and essential?" Asking yourself such questions can help you identify your first priority—what is the most important thing in your life—and to order everything accordingly.

In the movie *City Slickers*, a group of unhappy middle-aged New Yorkers go on a cattle drive to experience the West and seek happiness. When one of the men asks Curly, "What is the meaning of life?" the wise old cowhand responds, "Just one thing."[29] The men realize that they need to decide what is most important to them.

Viktor Frankl, a survivor of the Nazi work camps, discovered an important lesson in freedom while observing people who survived the loss of nearly everything. He found that the man who has discovered a person worthy of his love or a worthy purpose to serve cannot be held in chains.[30] Martin Luther King, Jr., expressed it this way:

> Even if he tries to kill you, *(He can't kill you)* you'll develop the inner conviction that there are some things so dear, some things so precious, some things so eternally true, that they are worth dying for. And . . . if a man has not discovered something that he will die for, he isn't fit to live.[31]

What is your "one thing"? What are your deepest desires, worthy of your sacrifice? What is the eternal truth that's worth dying for?

It is God himself. Everything else is oversold; God is the only One who exceeds our expectations in every way. God is very much like the wine that Jesus miraculously made from water in Cana: astonishing in quality, refreshing and pure, intoxicating and gracious. He is like the best wine saved for last, unexpectedly wonderful when all else has disappointed and faded.

Choosing God involves a paradox: *Complete surrender to God will actually make you free! Abandoning ourselves to him leads to abundant life.*

Why? Because the One we serve, sacrifice for, and love is Love itself. He is our highest good, and he always wants what is best for us. As Paul writes, "[N]ow that you have been set free from sin and have become slaves of God, the return you get is sanctification and its end, eternal life" (Romans 6:22).

If we were to be slaves of anything other than God, we would experience tyranny, deprivation, and loss. But being a slave to God unveils our true self, and the result is glory. Looking to

Jesus alone brings not deprivation but our true identity as sons and daughters of God.

We are like the burning bush that Moses saw in the desert: set on fire yet not consumed. This is a great image for the love of God in the human heart. We are purified by God's holy love, and we become complete in him.

One time God asked me to do something big. I was working part-time and had only a few hundred dollars in my bank account. A dear friend was engaged and very excited for her wedding, but she had no money for a dress. This young woman had experienced many traumas growing up. She had not known a stable home and at times was raised by foster parents.

My heart leapt at the opportunity to show my friend God's love. I went to the bank, emptied my account, and anonymously left her the money with a note explaining that it was for her wedding dress. At the time, it felt like a big sacrifice.

Now, over the years, I have made many decisions with money—some good and some foolish. This one I will never regret. Even though it required everything I had at the time, it was an expression of the values that God had placed in my heart, and it brought me joy. Thinking about that dress still makes me smile. This is the paradox of holiness: sacrifice and self-abandonment lead us to joy and fulfillment.

I hope that this short book has given you some clarity and direction about what it means to be holy and about how to pursue holiness. My desire is that many who read it will see their lives with a fresh hope. I believe that when we see ourselves as children of God, no longer bound by sin but embraced by love and mercy, we will be bold in the pursuit of holiness.

May the Spirit of Christ in you make you strong, that you might perceive the depths of God's love and say yes to the life of Jesus in you. Say yes to a sacrificial life, as Christ laid down his life for you. Say yes to a joyful life, filled with anticipation of future glory. With every choice, with every yes, let us embrace the love that has captured our hearts.

Prayer

God, you are my "One Thing." You are the fulfillment of my deepest desires. In you my heart finds peace and joy. Holy Spirit, I ask for you to reveal to me the obstacles and areas where I am bound. Help me to understand the tactics of my Enemy so that I might take my stand against them. Show me any resentments that I carry or deceptions that I have believed. I surrender my life into your hands. You are my healer and deliverer. Jesus, I trust in you.

REFLECTION QUESTIONS
(For Individual Use or with a Small Group)

1. Ask the Holy Spirit to reveal to you any lies that have kept you from living in freedom.

2. Write down anything from this chapter that has been a struggle for you. Take time to renounce these things, out loud, in the name of Jesus.

3. Practice using the Five Keys, allowing the Spirit to reveal your heart to you. Is there anyone you need to forgive? Do you need to repent for anything? Let the Spirit lead you.

4. Are you willing to give God everything? What would it look like to abandon yourself to him? Is there something that he is asking of you?

Epilogue

Neal Lozano

Each person has a unique personality and history through which God wants to display his glory to the world.

My cousin Fr. Michael Scanlan prayed with me many years ago, and my life was changed forever. He stepped in and drew close to our family when my dad died. He presided at our family weddings and Baptisms. He said Mass on our vacations.

Fr. Mike made an enormous contribution to the Church as the president of Franciscan University in Steubenville, Ohio. I don't know anyone who prayed more or was more eager to serve. He was just a man who made himself available to God. He was not some distant saint that I read about but rather a man living out his calling as best he could.

At Fr. Mike's funeral Mass, the arena was filled with people whose lives he had touched. His coffin was right in front of the altar, where the bread and wine would become the Body and Blood of Jesus. In a flash, I could see clearly that Fr. Mike had allowed Jesus to be made known, uniquely in time, through his life. Jesus had lived in him and through him. It was all about Jesus! To me, this is what holiness is all about.

I love books that present the truth simply and invite a personal response. *Free to Be Holy* has renewed my zeal to respond to God's invitation to holiness. This book reminds us that we have been made holy and can come to greater holiness by making ourselves available to God every moment of every day. We are called to be his witness, his instrument. We are to manifest the life of Jesus in our unique circumstances.

Is this a burden or a joy? It depends on how alive you are to the reality of what Jesus has done for you. If your focus has shifted from his mercy to what you have to do, then it will be a burden. Joy is found in the truth and the empowering presence of God, given to us in the Holy Spirit, where we find true freedom. "Now the Lord is the Spirit, and where the Spirit of the Lord is, there is freedom" (2 Corinthians 3:17). *Free to Be Holy* is aptly named.

Matt's life has been marked by zeal since he encountered Jesus in high school. His love for the Scriptures goes back even further. When Matt was ten years old, he stood up in front of our local Catholic community and said, "I just want to say that I love the Bible." You can see in Matt's writing this passion for God's word. He has taken a deep dive especially into the letters of St. Paul as a primary source for this work.

I wish I had had this book many years ago. I remember giving a talk at a men's retreat forty years ago. I spoke about these verses from the Letter to the Galatians:

For I through the law died to the law, that I might live to God. I have been crucified with Christ; it is no longer I who live, but Christ who lives in me; and the life I now live in the flesh I live by faith in the Son of God, who loved me and gave himself for me. (2:19-20)

I was in awe of St. Paul, that he no longer lived, but Christ lived in him. I shared with the men about how his life was worth imitating and learning from. But lurking in the background of these reflections was always a negative comparison. I thought that I would never be that holy. I thought that I could never say, "I no longer live, but it is Christ who lives in me."

Now I know that St. Paul is inviting us into the living reality of what God has done for us. We were made holy through the obedience of Jesus, by the offering of his blood (see Hebrews 13:12). St. Paul invites each of us to take a leap into this truth. This book echoes that invitation.

Free to Be Holy offers you a weapon of truth so that you can stand in your identity as a child of God. Through Baptism and faith, you have received the truth—that you have been crucified with Christ. You are God's workmanship. The plan of the Father is that you be sent into this world as a unique expression of his Son.

This pattern is manifest in Matt's life. As his father, I greatly delight in his life and his calling. I rejoice as I read and reread this book. My pleasure over him is a small reflection of the delight that our eternal Father has for all his children.

One of the greatest contributions of this book is the emphasis on the blood of Jesus. In the *Catechism* we read, "The human

"

Free to Be Holy offers you a weapon of truth so that you can stand in your identity as a child of God.

heart is converted by looking upon him whom our sins have pierced."[32] The *Catechism* then quotes Pope St. Clement I:

> Let us fix our eyes on Christ's blood and understand how precious it is to his Father, for, poured out for our salvation, it has brought to the whole world the grace of repentance.[33]

Recently, my pastor mentioned how unfortunate it is that we can no longer share the cup at Mass because of the Covid pandemic. I was touched by his passion for the Blood of Jesus. Following his talk, we had a time of reflection. I wanted to shout, "If we cannot drink the Blood, let's at least talk about it!"

Contemplating the blood of Christ deeply moves me. The old hymn "Nothing But the Blood" has moved me to tears. It feels like an arrow of God's love penetrating deeply into my heart. Here are a few of its lines:

> What can wash away my sin?
> Nothing but the blood of Jesus;
> What can make me whole again?
> Nothing but the blood of Jesus.
>
> Oh! precious is the flow
> That makes me white as snow;
> No other fount I know,
> Nothing but the blood of Jesus.[34]

Let us fix our eyes on Christ's blood.

Free to Be Holy can be a tool for parents and teachers to talk about the blood of Jesus, what he has done to make us holy, and how that is the foundation for a joyful life of growing in holiness.

Since reading *Free to Be Holy*, I have been consciously reminding myself that I am holy. By grace, holiness lives in me! This has affected me throughout the day, influencing my thinking and behavior.

I invite you to join me in remembering the message of this book, declaring that you have been made holy by his blood shed for us. If you have children, teach them that they are holy because the life of the Son of God has been poured out for them.

The Holy Spirit is at work in us, to bring us deeper into the freedom to walk in holiness. We find this freedom as we embrace our identity as the children of God. We all need to receive the Father's words of welcome, delight, and pleasure.

True holiness begins and ends in the Father's heart. Jesus' obedient sacrifice has made it possible for all to come to the Father without shame or fear and receive the treasure of his words of delight and pleasure. Thus we can experience a portion of the eternal embrace that awaits us, when we will meet Jesus face-to-face.

Notes

1. Pope John Paul II, *God Is Beauty: A Retreat on the Gospel and Art* (Downington, PA: Theology of the Body Institute Press, 2022), 58.
2. Pope John Paul II, 58.
3. *Catechism*, 2567.
4. *Catechism*, 773, citing Pope St. John Paul II, Apostolic Letter *Mulieris Dignitatem*, August 15, 1988, 27.
5. *Catechism*, 773, citing Ephesians 5:27.
6. Pope Benedict XVI, Lenten Message, 2007, www.vatican .va/content/benedict-xvi/en/messages/lent/documents/hf_ben-xvi_mes_20061121_lent-2007.html.
7. Deacon Frederick Bartels, "Francis, The Eucharist Is Our Spiritual Lifeblood," *Joy in Truth*, June 25, 2014, https:// joyintruth.com/pope-francis-the-eucharist-is-our-spiritual-lifeblood/.
8. *Catechism*, 1227, citing cf. 1 Corinthians 6:11; 12:13.
9. St. Faustina, *Divine Mercy in My Soul: The Diary of the Servant of God, Sister M. Faustina Kowalska* (Stockbridge, MA: Marian Press, 2005), xxii.
10. Mark Twain, *Personal Recollections of Joan of Arc by The Sieur Louis de Conte (Her Page and Secretary)* (San Francisco, CA: Ignatius Press, 1989), 341.
11. Thérèse of Lisieux, *Story of a Soul: The Autobiography of St. Thérèse of Lisieux* (Washington, DC: ICS Publications, 1975).
12. Anthony Showalter, "Leaning on the Everlasting Arms," 1887.

13. Charles H. Spurgeon, *The Complete Works of C. H. Spurgeon, Volume 29: Sermons 1698-1756* (Harrington, DE: Delmarva Publications, Inc., 2015), 513.

14. Robert Critchley, "My Hope Is Built on Nothing Less," 2007.

15. David Givey, *The Social Thought of Thomas Merton: The Way of Nonviolence and Peace for the Future* (Winona, MN: Saint Mary's Press, 2009), 12.

16. Common paraphrase of Catherine of Siena, from the original, "If you are what you ought to be, you will light a fire not only there but in all of Italy."

17. *The Catholic Encyclopedia*, "St. Thomas Aquinas," www.newadvent.org/cathen/14663b.htm.

18. Walter Isaacson, *Steve Jobs* (New York, NY: Simon and Schuster, 2011), 575.

19. Pope St. John Paul II, Homily at 17th World Youth Day, July 28, 2002, 5, https://www.vatican.va/content/john-paul-ii/en/homilies/2002/documents/hf_jp-ii_hom_20020728_xvii-wyd.html.

20. Aleksandr Solzhenitsyn, *The Gulag Archipelago 1918-1956: An Experiment in Literary Investigation, Volume 2* (New York, NY: Harper and Row, 1975), 28.

21. St. Ambrose, *Concerning Repentance*, bk. 2, chap. 10, §96, https://www.newadvent.org/fathers/34062.htm.

22. Corrie ten Boom, with John and Elizabeth Sherrill, *The Hiding Place* (Grand Rapids, MI: Baker Publsihing Group, 1971), 240.

23. St. Augustine of Hippo, *Confessions*, bk. 13, chap. 9, section 10.

24. Pope Francis, General Audience, May 2, 2018.

25. *Catechism* 2015, citing cf. Timothy 4.

26. See Charles Duhigg, *The Power of Habit: Why We Do What We Do in Life and Business* (New York, NY: Random House Trade Paperbacks, 2014).

27. John Michael Rziha, *Perfecting Human Actions: St. Thomas Aquinas on Human Participation in Eternal Law* (Washington, DC: The Catholic University of America Press, 2009), 257.

28. *The Lord of the Rings: The Two Towers,* directed by Peter Jackson (New Line Cinema, 2002).

29. *City Slickers,* directed by Ron Underwood (Nelson Entertainment, 1991).

30. See Victor Frankl, *Man's Search for Meaning: An Introduction to Logotherapy* (Boston, MA: Beacon Press, 1992).

31. Dr. Martin Luther King, Jr., speech in Detroit, Michigan, June 1963, https://www.mesaartscenter.com/download. php/engagement/jazz-a-to-z/resources/archive/2016-2017/ teacher-resources/speech-at-the-great-march-detroit.

32. *Catechism*, 1432, citing cf. John 19:37; Zechariah 12:10.

33. *Catechism*, 1432, citing St. Clement of Rome, Epistle to the Corinthians 7, 4, in J. P. Migne, *Patrologia Graeca* 1, 224.

34. Robert Lowry, "Nothing But the Blood," 1876, https:// library.timelesstruths.org/music/Nothing_but_the_Blood/.

Heart of the Father Ministries: Unbound Ministry

Everyone is fighting an invisible battle.

Some of us battle to overcome negative patterns of thinking, secret sins, and unhealthy dynamics in relationships. Others wrestle with small and big deceptions, as well as feelings of hopelessness and anxiety.

Unbound ministry releases the power of Jesus into wounded hearts.

Unbound is a ministry of healing and freedom that helps people to break free from their spiritual bondage. Unbound gives people the opportunity to tell their stories in a safe and loving environment, surrender to God's power, offer forgiveness to others, and to experience God's tender love.

The Five Keys of Unbound Ministry

- Repentance and Faith
- Forgiveness
- Renunciation
- Authority
- The Father's Blessing

When these Five Keys are applied to a person's story in an Unbound ministry session, the power of Jesus is released to heal and set them free.

Heart of the Father Ministries is equipping the Church with Unbound ministry, proclaiming the transforming power of the gospel in a darkened world.

Unbound ministry brings healing to our emotional, sexual, physical, and spiritual wounds.

"A young man came up to me and said he needed prayer. He told me he was battling addiction and was full of anger. As I lead him through Unbound, he was able to forgive those who had hurt him and renounce anger and other spirits. He found me two weeks later, and with much joy in his face and color in his cheeks, he thanked me for praying with him. He said he was free of anger and because of this new freedom, he had hope that he would be able to get off of drugs and have a normal life."

—Therese from Maryland

Unbound: Freedom in Christ Conferences

The Unbound: Freedom in Christ Conference is the signature event that introduces people to Unbound ministry. This 2-3-day event includes a series of talks presented to a large group, usually between 150-300 attendees. During the conference, we present the message of the Five Keys and share inspiring testimonies about how God has set people free. The ministry team provides several opportunities throughout the conference for attendees to receive ministry using the Five Keys.

Unbound Basic Training

Basic Ministry Training is a valuable experience for anyone who wants to be able to offer Unbound ministry.

Unbound Advanced Training

As a follow-up to the Basic Training, the Unbound Advanced Ministry Training equips people who are doing Unbound ministry and desire to grow in effectiveness as a leader, intercessor, trainer, or ministry leader. The Advanced Training is also offered as a Study Program (DVD and Workbook).

Clergy Retreats and Workshops

Heart of the Father offers several events specifically designed to help those in pastoral ministry. These retreats and workshops help those in full-time ministry to experience Unbound and receive the training they need while enjoying fellowship with other ministers.

For more information, visit www.heartofthefather.com

Resources to Get You Started with Unbound Ministry

Despite our best efforts, many of us struggle with sinful patterns of thinking and behaving. Our lack of freedom leaves us feeling hopeless. Author Neal Lozano shows us how to tap into the power of the gospel that sets us free. In *Unbound*, you will discover the keys to freedom. Neal lays out a strategy for overcoming the tactics of the Enemy and discovering freedom in the Father's love. Balanced and hopeful, *Unbound* will help you to start living the abundant, glorious life God has in mind.

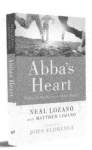

Do you know your heavenly Father's heart? Our heart's deepest need is to experience the love and mercy of God the Father. *Abba's Heart* is a powerful invitation to know God as our Father and experience His love, lavished on us in Christ. Come home to the Father today!

Made in the USA
Monee, IL
26 May 2024